Someone Stole My Outhouse

...and other tales of home improvement

Someone Stole My Outhouse

...and other tales of home improvement

By

Cindy Bellinger

Library of Congress Card Number: 00-112335
ISBN #0-944383-54-8

Cover Design by Don Strel

Illustrations by Peggy Warren

High-Lonesome Books
P.O. Box 878
Silver City, NM 88062

DEDICATION

First, this book is for my father who let me play with all his hammers, saws and pliers and taught me how to sand, paint and stain.

Next, it's for all the other men who have showed me another thing or two about building—Frank, Dave, Ed, George, Truel, Dodge, Clark, Reid, Art, Mick, Jack, Steve, Ernesto, and Kenny.

And finally, this book is also for my mother who taught me not to be afraid of hard work.

Table of Contents

Introduction

Cindy's home improvement column has grown so popular at *The New Mexican* that in the off weeks when it doesn't run I take calls from readers wondering where it is. Many tell me they've never picked up a hammer in their life. They read Cindy because her writing has the simple gift of speaking to us and making us laugh.

She lives in Pecos, NM (pop. 1,100). Ask for directions to her house and you'll get the typical country lingo: go past the one stop sign in town and head into the canyon. Then you climb a steep gravel road that looks as if it just heads off into the forest. Her house is on the right—the one with the piles of wood, fencing, scrap metal and other artifacts that years ago had seen better days.

In terrain split by one of the best trout rivers left in the American West, Cindy lives in a place that backs up to the National Forest and a collapsed chicken coop. For some, the ambiance might be a bit on the rustic side. For Cindy, it's a venue that embodies the passion in all of us to do better. And Cindy has done much to make her home better. From the colored marbles cemented in her stone wall, to the spice rack, kitchen counter, new closet doors and tiled bathroom.

For many, the handiwork Cindy writes about is beyond us. For others, it is within reach given the right tools, the right do-it-yourself book, and the right inspiration at the right time of day. Of course it helps to have the needed materials when all the other things come together and so having as much stuff stockpiled and available is, of course, a virtue in Cindy's world.

"Now, there's nothing I love more than junk wood, unless it's how that wood comes to me," she writes. "I'm not sure when scrounging for wood took hold of me, but I've always enjoyed making a haul...Once I squealed to a halt and grabbed a wooden crate from the middle of the highway. It splintered beautifully and made great kindling."

Cindy has never weighed in on the bevy of home-improvement shows that fill the airwaves: the ones that often end with perfect doors, matching molding and impaled self-confidence. Instead she writes about her missing outhouse, a failed porch project, how repairing a roof builds community, and how she sometimes gets so frustrated with projects she has to just stop and play with her cat, Mr. Ames.

And even though Cindy really does know how to use a miter box, hang doors, and load a staple gun, she struggles with the muses of home remodeling and puts off projects well into the next season and sometimes that's just as well.

"The other day I trimmed my new Virginia Creeper, cutting the dead tendrils," she writes in an essay on curb appeal, even though she lives in a part of the world that shuns such amenities. "Like a nit-wit, though, I trimmed the one tendril I meant to train up a post. My garden survives in spite of me."

Cindy's trials, missteps, and frustrations as well as her virtue in being able to laugh and try again—or not try again—has truly taken the readers of *The New Mexican*. It all started when together we came up with the idea of doing a one-time feature about her own remodeling. After it ran, we decided to do another and the rest is history. Cindy speaks to those who do work on their own houses, to those who might give it a try one of these days, and to those who may never use a handsaw let alone an electric one. The refreshing slant about Cindy's home improvement column is she speaks without the straight-line character of a Martha Stewart.

It was Wallace Stegner who extolled, "Find a place, dig in and defend it."

It is Cindy Bellinger who best writes about that "digging in" on a plot of forest land in Northern New Mexico.

Bruce Krasnow, Assistant City Editor, *The Santa Fe New Mexican*

Chapter 1

There's Always Another Project

My ability to measure must have gotten stuck somewhere around third grade. I can measure something three times and come up with three different measurements. This doesn't bode well when I'm putting up shelves or paneling the walls. A fairly substantial woodpile of mistakes sits by the back door. But if I don't burn the pieces they'll probably come in handy for the next project.

And there is always a next project.

I'm one of those unusual women who likes remodeling her own house. I've always been this way and, renting or owning, have rarely left a house or apartment untouched. I've painted ceilings, patched holes in walls, re-varnished old wooden floors, secured shelves in closets, built stone walls. Twice I've lived in brand new houses only to feel restless after awhile because there wasn't anything to do, nothing to fix.

So over a year ago I entered heaven. I bought a little shack that needed just a bit of revising. The toilet had leaked for at least twenty years and all the floorboards were rotten. The burnt-orange shag carpet from the '70s had to go. The yellowed ceilings needed painting and the hideous fake wood paneling needed covering. The entire undertaking looked pretty overwhelming.

Because few boundaries in life appeal to me, I'm drawn to open living spaces. So a room more the size of a closet quickly got put on the demolition list. I'd never torn down a wall before and my approach was a little tentative. Until I learned my ex-boyfriend wasn't going to pay me the $6,500 as he had agreed. I seized a sledgehammer and that wall came tumbling down.

I had a notion about what needed to be done with the rotten floorboards, but was at a loss as to where to start. Then a carpenter friend took on the job. I worked alongside him, learning to use a screw gun and how to snap a chalk line—a handy mark if you can measure right. I helped rip plywood and cut drywall. Then he showed me how to put up insulation, and I quickly learned why he so willingly let me do it. I've never scratched so much in my life.

The day all the pipes and drains were open and the so-called plumber finally admitted he didn't know what he was doing, I fired him and found another who knew his job. As an added bonus, he turned out to be reliable and fair. Later we even worked out a trade—my old washer for a few more hookups.

Then came the electrical work, which is beyond me. I can barely get flashlight batteries in right. Another friend is an electrician so we worked out another trade: switches, outlets and motion detectors in exchange for editing his book.

And then they all left. Before the faucets could be connected in the bathroom, the counter needed tiling. The shower needed tiling. Shelves needed building. This all meant many trips to the hardware stores. Being a woman and shopping for vise grips or bags of cement brings a few raised eyebrows and periodically some rather rude remarks.

If possible, I go to Empire Builders where no one yet has been condescending; and the guys at Big Jo True Value Hardware are most respectful. If I can't find what I need at these places, though, I'm forced to go to that other store. You know the one—where you get more help from the other customers than the sales staff. The one where no matter what you want, they're out. It's the one place in town where a man in the lumberyard actually told me I couldn't build shelves because I was a "f------- woman." You leave the place feeling like you've been in a car wreck.

Still, I like hardware stores; and it all began in my father's garage. He built the house I grew up in and his tool collection offered endless hours of play. Many of his chisels and hand drills came from my maternal grandfather and great grandfather, who were both carpenters. A few years after my father died, I helped clean out his garage and now have luscious wooden handled screwdrivers, awls, and an old rasp has become my favorite since a lot of my boards need a bit of evening out. Another favorite is a small well-worn pry bar. It's great for ripping out trim, pulling nails and basic general destruction.

My work doesn't come close to being professional, but nothing gives a feeling of a job well done as doing it myself. Which is probably why I'm always nosing around for another project, as my ex-husband so bitterly pointed out. He was a mechanical engineer, and I guess got tired of holding the ends of boards. But he did teach me how to put in molly bolts, use a router and feel comfortable with power tools. After we got divorced, I bought a circular saw of my own and never looked back.

For all the stains and cuts on my hands, one would think I'd be more skilled than I am. It's probably because I push myself, taking on bigger projects than I'm capable of, that I never seem to arrive at some level of competence. Sometimes I'm even forced into new arenas.

After tiling the bathroom counter recently, I called the plumber to tell him the faucets could be connected. No playing the helpless female with him; he's seen me pour a footer for a wall. "Oh, you can do it yourself," he said and went on to describe the parts I'd need. I also couldn't convince another friend that I'm helpless.

Needing more help installing a new kitchen faucet, I called him up. Instead of running over to save the day he, too, gave instructions over the phone. Frustrated and feeling way over my head, I did finally get it in. "There was never any doubt in my mind you could do it," he said. So now I can add basic plumbing to the list.

Problem is with each accomplishment my confidence grows along with my curiosity. Lately I've been wondering how difficult adding on would be. I've done all the steps, just not all at once. And more and more I'm catching myself eyeing the living room wall. Of course, I wouldn't stop there. It'd be great to make the sunroom two stories.

Problem is there's always another project.

Chapter 2

The Queen of Spice Racks

A corner in the kitchen has bothered me from the day I moved in. No matter how I looked at it, the amount of wasted space couldn't be ignored. The area quickly got put on the revision list, but as more urgent projects came up, that particular corner kept slipping to the bottom of the list—until my oven died.

The morning I turned on the oven and a half-hour later got so dizzy I had to hold onto a chair, I knew it was time to get a new stove. Gratefully this meant demolishing the corner cabinet I'd also wanted to replace. I began by moving all the pots and pans to the living room; and since my workshop is awfully cold these days, my tools have gravitated to the kitchen. I stood back and heaved a heavy sigh.

This is the first law of home improvement: mess with one corner and the entire house gets thrown into chaos.

It took about ten seconds to level the cabinet, the wood was so old. In fact, I didn't even have to back the screws out; they just pulled out of the wall. Then after my plumber disconnected the gas line and whisked away the stove, the resulting hole in the kitchen opened a lot of possibilities. But first things first. Throughout the house I'm paneling all the walls one stained board at a time. It's a slow process, but when I heard myself say, "I'll just snap on some boards," I knew I was in trouble.

Ever hear carpenters talk? They "pop off" nails. They "hang" drywall. They "rip out" a floor. The colorful language and free-wheeling euphemisms cleverly disguise hours of work. The one that really gets me is "throwing on a coat of paint." If you've ever painted anything, you know it involves a lot more than throwing. And as I started tapping around for studs in the kitchen wall, I knew a lot more than "snapping on a few boards" would be needed.

In one area there wasn't anything to attach the boards to, which meant using molly bolts, which meant dragging out the drill and bits and extension cords and rummaging through all my nuts and bolts hoping to avoid a trip to the store. And because I don't have three hands the project took all day. By the time the boards were in place, I was sounding like an entire construction crew.

With the paneling up, I now could do some serious planning. What I needed most was a spice rack. Living too long with jars scattered on the counter, I'd tried pretending I wouldn't have to make another one. The last three places I've lived, I ended up custom designing a spice rack that perfectly contoured the exact space. I'd been avoiding another one because they're not easy. I mean, fitting small pieces of wood between even smaller pieces of wood requires exact measuring and close cutting. I tend to go for the big picture and get snagged on the details. Recently a friend passed on a hint, though. Use a sharp pencil and cut outside the line. It's helping. My ratio of botched boards is definitely going down.

Putting them all together is another problem. I live alone and my schedule is rather odd so I end up taking a few minutes to work on projects before heading out each day. With no one around to hold the ends of boards I've endured countless hours of amazing contortions trying to do it myself.

One time several years ago when making one of my famous spice racks, I struggled to hold everything while screwing the pieces together. I needed about eight more hands and the frustration brought me to the edge of tears. I even pleaded to the gods for some help. Then low and behold suddenly all the pieces lined up long enough to get fastened. Within minutes it was done. Only in Santa Fe do we have New Age construction angels.

But now I live in Pecos and I'm beginning to think the gods don't extend this far. Take the other day. Putting up a new calendar, I held the nail, heaved back on the hammer and slammed down on my thumb. And if this was with a hammer, think of the near misses I've had with chainsaws and axes.

But as I headed to the lumberyard for spice rack wood I was kind of excited. The kitchen was finally going to be fixed up and any moment a shipment would arrive. For years I've wanted a new set of drill bits. I'm still using the ones I bought in '74 when, during a lecture at a women's lib gathering, the speaker expounded on how we had to begin acquiring tools. I had no idea she meant emotional and career building tools. I went out and bought a drill.

After poking around town for a new set of bits recently, a friend gave me a discount tool catalog. Since choosing country living over city dwelling, I've become a catalog shopper. More, perhaps, because I like opening packages. But some things are definitely cheaper. Like the exact bits are half what any place in town is selling them for. And I don't have to stand in the checkout line.

Anyway, with measurements in my head I went to the store looking for the straightest lengths, an impossible task at best. What happens with all those boards that curve so far out of straight they could be used for modern sculptures? After dismissing all but a few, I headed home.

And once again began wrangling small pieces of wood between even smaller pieces of wood. Forgetting, of course, to measure how many jars would fit on a shelf and not planning enough shelves. I quickly remembered why I didn't want to make another spice rack. At some point I always have to start over.

Chapter 3

Addiction: Building Shelves

Some people are addicted to wine and old movies. Some can't get enough sex. Or food. Or exercise. For myself I'm obsessed with making shelves. This, of course, has nothing to do with my huge collection of books. It probably was not wise to take a temporary job at a local bookstore. Right after I started, I had to put up two more shelves in the bedroom. However, leaving the bookstore did nothing to lessen my book buying sprees. The piles of books kept growing, and I kept wondering how to get one more shelf.

Using brackets, blocks of wood and corbels, I've attached shelves over doorways, along windowsills, and inside closets. Once I even fastened a clever make-shift rack on the side of an end table. My main shelving system, though, consists of bricks and boards. Having moved about twenty times in the last ten years, this seemed a most reasonable way to go. Yet when visiting other people's houses I always find myself hungering for their built-in shelves. They look so substantial, so permanent.

No doubt it was the luscious idea of permanency that made me begin eyeing a certain wall in my living room. Years ago a sunroom had been added, and with the windows still in place the wall was virtually useless. After buying the place, I hung a Persian rug over the windows and let it go at that.

Then a few weeks ago I felt it coming. If you're a chocoholic, you know the feeling, those early signs of a sudden craving. It starts with a distant hum and intensifies until you just have to make a batch of chocolate chip cookies. The need for another bookshelf starts the same way. First, a vague idea floats in. Then plans start forming. Pictures get scribbled on scraps of paper. And before you know it you're figuring the number of boards. Now, whether I like it or not, I'm in the middle of a serious bookshelf-making binge.

At first I thought about copying my one free-standing bookcase. When I taught English in a small town, a shop class made it for me. Some of the spacing is wrong and too many books have to lie flat, but the kids were enthusiastic and it's become a treasure. Because of it, my plan evolved into two bookcases about six feet apart with boards placed between them for long shelves.

Of course, the day I planned to take out the windows and replace them with insulation, everyone disappeared on me. All my friends found better things to do. Imagine. So I set out alone. And the first thing I did, while staining the boards, was absent-mindedly set the can on my car. It left a brown ring, complete with drips from the paintbrush. It's an old car and I'll probably be its last owner, so all I did was laugh, remembering the time my father actually hand painted his old Pontiac Chief.

My father was a boat painter back in the days before fiberglass put him and his kind out of business. He kept hundreds of gallons of paint in the garage. And one Saturday when he went to find something to paint his car with, well, there was a whole lot of bottom gray.

We lived in a small town and by Monday morning word had spread. Junior high is not a good time for one of your parents to make a spectacle of himself, and I got a good dose of teasing. I braved it all with a smile and thirty-five years later decided to leave the ring of brown stain on my car as homage to a family tradition.

It's a good thing I like the rustic look. I knew the shelves would have that "Old World" appeal right from the beginning. I'm not a finish carpenter, probably because nothing ever gets finished. Also, since I do not possess any innate sense of physics or engineering, I'm afraid I might be in for replaying another family event. I was in my early twenties and visiting my mother one afternoon, when we heard a horrible crash in the back room. After thirty years four rows of shelves had finally given in, pulled loose from their bearings and collapsed. I have no idea if my current structure will hold up or not. I figure if it lasts thirty days I may be OK.

What worries me more is what I'll do when a shelf-building craze starts again. I've run out of wall space. Maybe I'll have to switch addictions and lie back, eat chocolate and read some of my books.

Chapter 4

The Rasping Secret

It's been several weeks and the saga of my shelf building addiction continues. In the beginning I threw myself into the project, but as often happens, I got overwhelmed. Especially after counting all the pieces. Imagine eighty-seven pieces of 2x2s and 1x12s, not to mention the mounds of assorted screws. I couldn't face it. So I did what I've always done when a project gets way over my head. I threw a party.

Years ago when I bought a double-wide, I had a skirting party. About fifteen people showed up ostensibly to build a skirt around the bottom of the home. But some sure spent an awful lot of time around the pizza and cooler. Another time I had a deck erecting party. It happened to be the hottest day of the year. Still, I barbecued some chicken we're still talking about.

So with this history already established, the other day I had a shelf-raising. We don't have many barns around here so this was the best I could do. I spread the word and by the time the day arrived only two people showed up. They've been to all my building extravaganzas. Said they couldn't wait for another. However, I think, my bribe of chocolate chip cookies helped. I've known Becky and Clark forever. When they moved here five years ago, I was delighted. Becky became my best friend in sixth grade; she met Clark in junior college and they've been together ever since.

I've always been amazed at Clark's dexterity. He's an artist and when they moved here, he set about building a studio. I didn't know he could do that. I'm always amazed how guys just seem to know how to build a house or repair a car or rewire a toaster. Seems I have to struggle just to hold a hammer.

When I first proposed the project, Clark asked for a fax of my design. That done, word came back that I needed to go to art school. I couldn't help it if my bookcases ended up looking like they had wings. But once we got into the swing of things, Clark said, "This is a really good design." That pleased me. I mean, I'd thought about it for a long time.

The first thing we did was wonder why the bookcase was off by half an inch. All the braces leveled out. The two sideboards measured evenly. Becky and I decided it had to be the ceiling throwing in an optical illusion. But Clark summed it up better: "It has to do with making squares on a round planet."

We settled into a routine: Clark cut the boards, Becky and I screwed them together. In their collection of tools they'd brought two Makitas and I had mine. The running question became: how many Makitas does it take to put up shelves? At times three still weren't enough. We pre-drilled holes, drove in screws. Becky would hand me one drill only to be instantly ready with another. Clearly, she'd done this before.

Then some of the braces proved a little long. Clark said he'd take them out and cut off the ends. Becky and I had a better idea. Rasp them. Clark, totally against it, said it wouldn't look right. But our way was quicker. When Clark was outside, I grabbed my trusty heavy-duty rasp and went to work. "Quick, here he comes," Becky would whisper. I'd hide the rasp and we went on drilling. He'd go back out on the porch and we'd rasp some more. That's the girl's way of doing it: just get it done. Becky and I have been giggling together for thirty-seven years.

What's so fun about doing your own work is watching an idea you've had for so long slowly begin to take shape. At one point I actually imagined walking through the living room without winding around piles of books on the floor. It'd be a whole new lifestyle.

After six hours the shelves were done. And the living room carpet was done in with sawdust, mud, screws and bits of cookie. Another thing about doing it yourself is the instant memories built in. I'll forever be pleased knowing that some of the edges rasped in secret work just fine.

Chapter 5

Something Loves A Stone Wall

You can thank me for the recent luscious rains. I didn't do a rain dance, just did what I do every spring: resume work on my stone wall. Sure enough, after I got another level of rocks mortared in, the rains began. First a light drizzle. Then a little harder. Then something like a torrent swooshed down, making me scramble around for tarps and a shovel. I did what I could, but diverting a steady rush of water bent on undermining all my work, not to mention my house, is not easy.

From the kitchen window, I begrudgingly watched small streams of gray run into the flower bed, over the flagstone walk and settle in a pool six inches deep by the front door.

Though the rain was certainly welcome, I crossed my fingers for the sun to return. However, hours later a new tributary of the Pecos River had cut through my garden. At that point I only sighed, remembering—

Something there is that doesn't love a stone wall...

In his poem "Mending Wall" Robert Frost finds the insistent prodding of nature keeps stones where they belong: on the ground. They have no business being part of property lines, and every winter the frozen ground swells—

And spills the upper boulders in the sun.

Frost works with a neighbor every spring to replace the fallen stones. Every spring I start my project anew. This doesn't mean I have to start over. With concrete, previous work stays pretty much intact. I just clean off the caked mud and continue.

I build my walls in fits and starts. It only takes an hour or so to mix up a batch of mortar and lay in some more stone. I can set a row in the morning and be ready for the world by noon. For years, it's been one of my favorite projects. I'm attracted to the solidity of concrete, the firmness of stones and the whimsy of sticking marbles and polished rocks in the mortar. I also stick in shells, bits of broken tile and now that I find them everywhere I walk in Pecos, I'm also adding fossils.

Something there is I love about stone walls.

Yet for some reason every wall I worked on in the past involved some emotional incident. When my now ex-husband and I began rebuilding a stone planter near the porch, a huge fight erupted. Over what, I can't remember. He walked off in a huff and I ended up finishing the job.

Another time after becoming engaged, I suggested making a stone flower bed on the east side of his house. I envisioned a low curved planter to catch the early sun. But this didn't go over very well either, and I realized he was more in love with the idea of being married than really being that way.

So when I finally bought a little plot of land with a perfect place for a stone wall, it looked heavenly. No hassles. No fights. A clear road ahead. Then the rains came.

I dug the foundation. Rain filled it up with mud. I poured the foundation; it became a soupy mess. I decided to wait for the rainy season to stop. Well into a drought, I got up early one morning to beat the sun. I mixed a batch for another pour. The drought broke that afternoon. Unprecedented precipitation, the headlines read. It's almost guaranteed now. I work on my stone wall, we'll get rain.

Surely, like Frost found, there's a poem here. And some morning I'll sit in the early sun in the patio on the east side of the house, flowers draping over the curved retaining wall, and begin writing it. If the rains don't come.

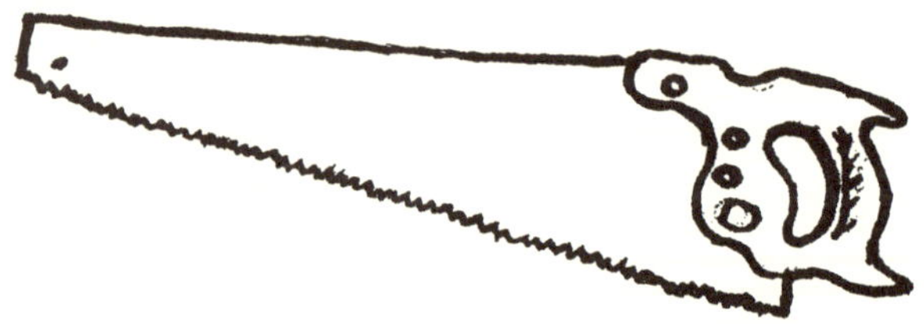

Chapter 6

Cement and the Five Year Old

Recently someone asked how long ago I started working with cement.

"It's not very usual for a woman to do that," he said. Maybe not, but when I was five it seemed perfectly OK.

One Sunday when I was in kindergarten I watched my father mix up a batch of mortar to patch a few cracks in the driveway. Seemed pretty easy. So the next day when I got off the bus, I went to work. Got a spoon, my beach pail and started the hose. My father kept a small pile of sand in the corner of the patio and a bag of cement in a corner of the brick barbecue.

Squatting down and mixing, I remember having a great time. Then I carried my little bucket to the sidewalk. And proceeded to fill all the cracks. I think it had something to do with not wanting to break my mother's back.

I worked very studiously, patting the mixture smooth with the curve of my spoon. After one crack got filled, I went to the next. I filled the cracks left by the concrete forms; I filled the cracks created by tree roots. I worked all afternoon.

And then I got in trouble. "I'm going to tell your father when he gets home," my mother promised. But Daddy tried hiding his smile when he heard what I'd done.

And those cracks stayed filled until five years ago, when the city came along and repaired the sewer lines.

For some reason I've always had an affinity for concrete, and one time when I was married my husband took on the task of making a high retaining wall in the back yard. He built the forms, was ready to go and rented a mixer. Only he couldn't get a good mix, so I took over. We worked out a great routine—me shoveling the mix, him pouring.

Another time I hired out a foundation pour and the contractor didn't order enough yards. The next pour looked somewhat suspicious, so I called the company that mixed it. Sure enough, to cut corners he'd ordered a less-than-adequate strength. I told him I wouldn't pay till I was satisfied. The day the mobile home arrived, the foundation cracked. I didn't pay.

A good friend travels widely and always brings me back a rock, something I requested from the start. One time she returned from Italy and handed me a gray clump. When I asked what it was, she told me it was part of an early Roman concrete wall. They used shells for lime and they were still intact.

Knowing her like I do, I asked, "Did you steal this?" Sheepishly, she nodded. It's become one of my most treasured mementos.

I spend a few hours every week working for a nonprofit foundation that preserves old buildings. It's turned out to be a great resource. Many of the board members and committee members are architects and contractors, if not serious do-it-yourselfers.

One day I asked Jack, one of the board members, about a concrete problem. Is there a way to tone down the gray? I wondered.

"Get some pigment," he said.

I had no idea. I also had no idea what problems adding a little color to my mixes would cause. First, I didn't know how much. The instructions came in French and German and something that looked like Sanskrit. Second, I didn't know when to mix it—dry or wet. Jack said wet. Steve said dry. Geez.

I finally trusted the five year old in me to figure it out, and set about playing with something that looked a lot like mud. Only it didn't hold. The next day all the rocks in my rock wall that I'd set so carefully came loose. I tried again, this time adding less sand.

Same thing.

"The pigment is probably acrylic-based," Steve said. "It takes longer to dry. Don't wiggle the rocks for several days." He knows how impatient I get.

It worked. Now my stone flowerbeds have that Old World look, not that sharp gray the early Romans had.

Chapter 7

Curb Appeal

Ask any realtor and they'll tell you keeping up curb appeal is essential to keeping up a house. But what happens if you don't have a curb? As I watered my meager garden the other day and noticed the continued growth of weeds, I thought maybe I ought to put in a curb. Not that I plan to sell anytime soon. But even a small boundary might help delineate things.

My land backs onto the National Forest, and as far as I can tell the forest doesn't really care where it leaves off and I begin. Seems I spend half my time hacking back encroaching brambles. If I'd let it, I'm sure the forest would gladly use my garden as underbrush to start a whole new stand of pines.

As it is, I'm trying my hardest to maintain my little plot of domestication. This hasn't been easy. First, ceramists could fill buckets of that micaceous clay touted so highly in these parts. Second, adobe brick enthusiasts couldn't go wrong, either. Third, I don't think any gardening book has taken my place into consideration. There is no zone that seems to apply. And it doesn't help that my perennials die off and my annuals return. Not knowing exactly what will take hold doesn't make for easy planning.

But when my garden started sprouting forth this spring, I was pleased until everything started blooming. The total array leaned toward blue. I love blue. But gardens need variety, and I tried. I really did.

Last year I set off for the nurseries armed with a list of what I wanted. Surely, staff members at the various nurseries would help me. Such ideals. High school kids just looked blank when I asked for Veronica. “She don’t work here,” I was told. My problems compounded when I encountered help who couldn’t speak English. I don’t know the Spanish word for pansy, so I tried Latin, a more universal language among gardeners. It was all Greek to them.

Finally, it’s not uncommon to walk through the humid, rich smelling green houses in town and see wonderful trays of lush growth. With no labels. Even more, as I’m learning this year, the ones with pictures of red and yellow flowers aren’t entirely accurate. I trusted the little pictures and expected a bright bouquet right outside my kitchen window. I got it. In blue and purple.

When all those big orange poppies burst full flavor all around town this year, I thought they’d be perfect to offset some of this blue. So I’m eager to get some going. Only with my luck I’ll get a mutated orange poppy that bursts into lavender.

I’ve always been captivated by gardens, and at five I had a fine eye for color, if not a grand entrepreneurial spirit. I’d seen a picture of a Parisian flower cart that truly caught my imagination, so one morning I took my little red wagon and blithely went around the block cutting all the flowers. Every single one. When my cart was ready, I set up business on the corner. Clearly, I’d moved beyond lemonade stands. But to say the least, the neighbors were not pleased.

Another time in the 5th grade and in a dither over the boy next door, I sat down in front of my mother's famed patch of daisies. Attempting divination, I pulled every petal off every yellow daisy wanting to know if he loved me or not. I never did find out. But to this day my mother never fails to remind me that her daisies never came back.

Some days my gardening techniques still haven't advanced much beyond decimation. The other day I trimmed my new very small Virginia Creeper, cutting the dead tendrils. And like a nit-wit I trimmed the one tendril I meant to train up a post. My garden survives in spite of me.

And I suppose if you came around the bend and saw the potted geraniums on the porch, the yarrow in the rock garden and the woolly thyme lusciously covering everything in its path, you might be pleasantly surprised. My little patch in the forest is actually starting to flourish. You might even call it curb appeal. Even without the curb.

Chapter 8

Ah, One More Tool

Well, I was there. Opening day of Home Depot. I don't usually join the hoards to grand openings, but this one I couldn't pass up. My last venture to "that other store" one evening turned typically grim. So along with hundreds of other people I showed up—amidst a collective sigh of relief.

Rumors had flown for years that Home Depot was coming to town, and those rumors always gathered momentum as people waited in very slow, very long lines at "that other store." Now all our waiting has paid off. The only problem I see is having to put your life on the line driving down Cerrillos Road to get there. But it may be a better trade-off than arriving peacefully at "that other store" and leaving ready to kill.

I wandered the aisles of Home Depot, gaping at the incredible amount of stuff. The manager said there's nearly 40,000 stocked items—and he promises to keep the shelves filled. I watched people ogling levels and wrenches, wire gates and kitchen counters. And I had a hunch I wasn't the only one conjuring up another project just for an excuse to buy another tool.

Actually, I thought I was the only one this devious until a few weeks ago when I journeyed down to Albuquerque to see my friend, Kenny. He's putting up fencing, installing a shed, getting soil ready to transplant a tree. When I arrived, he could have been doing any number of things.

But there he was. Nearly buried in leaves and branches high in the neighbor's tree. And that's when I met Lucille and Modesto—and learned about hidden desires for one more tool.

Lucille and I watched—holding our breath, rolling our eyes—as these men wielded chainsaws aboard wobbly 60-foot extension ladders. I've known Kenny a hundred years and know he's not as young as he used to be. It's one of those projects I would have hired out.

But when Modesto said he should have gotten one of those long handled electric tree pruners, that's when Lucille informed me the real reason for suddenly pruning the tree.

"He thinks up these projects just so he can buy another tool," she said, not even in a quiet aside. I could tell it was one of those hinges in a marriage, a point brought up again and again, swinging back and forth in argument, in affection.

"I can't tell you the number of times Mo's decided the backyard needed something new. We now have a large concrete slab out back. I don't know what for, but we have it."

Then she showed me inside the house, telling me how each room used to be. He'd enlarged the kitchen and added a sunroom off their bedroom.

"He got so many tools he had to build a shed to keep them in," Lucille said.

Back outside she told me Mo was going to rent a tractor soon to move some dirt, and Kenny had agreed to take the dirt for the continuing project in his yard. When I heard this, I thought, oh boy.

Lucille must have read my thoughts, "You know, boys with their tractors."

I knew. And remembered one time when I was married. My husband decided we had to have a basement. Which, of course, required a backhoe. Which, of course, he'd always wanted to try using. The operative word here is try.

The day he brought it home and began digging under the house, Jason, the three year old next door came over to help me watch. It took about a minute before Jason quietly tugged on my arm.

"He doesn't know what he's doing, does he?" Ah, the perception of three year olds. Gratefully, the job was finally hired out.

I had to leave in the middle of the tree pruning, only to hear later that the young twenty year old from across the street finally offered his assistance. He also must have been cringing at the sight of these old men flailing around. Thank goodness. Some jobs are best left to the young.

The saddest part is Mo didn't get to buy his long handled electric tree pruner. But he'll soon get to work a tractor. I'll definitely show up for that one. And I'm sure Kenny will put me to work spreading the dirt and digging in his new garden.

But, you know, I haven't seen a spade shovel in Kenny's collection of gardening tools. His birthday's coming up and it'd be the perfect present. Besides, walking the aisles of Home Depot the other day got that urge going—that urge to buy another tool. And making it a present satisfies all kinds of things. I can spend money on a tool and not feel the least bit of guilt. Isn't it amazing the contortions we go through to justify yet another tool?

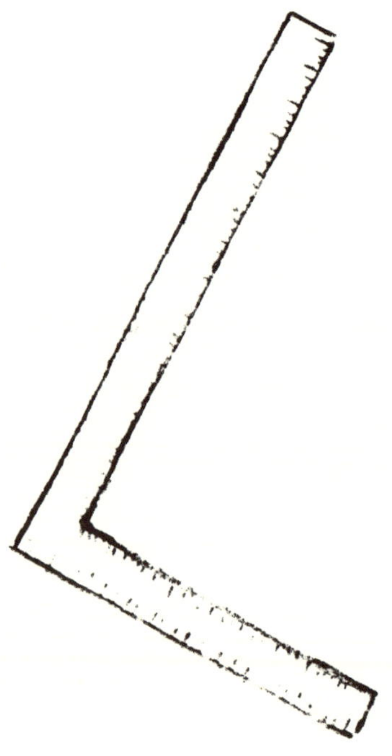

Chapter 9

On the Road to Destruction

I must have been about fifteen when a teacher said something about destruction coming before creation. I didn't get it. It took years of messing around with hammers and saws before I figured there might be some truth in it. As my projects kept getting bigger and bigger, the more destruction there was. I'm not sure anything creative ever followed, but if you make enough of mess at least it feels like you've done something.

No project, though, wrecks havoc like taking raw land and turning it into something civilized. Not long ago I hooked up with a former roommate, Anne, who suddenly had thirty-three very raw acres on her hands. She wanted to build a house and retire there someday.

"Come help me figure out what to do first," she wailed long distance.

Now this wasn't some small trek down the county road. Those thirty-three acres were in Nova Scotia. But raw land is raw land no matter where you are. It's the difference in terrain that throws you. I'm a Western girl, used to seeing miles and miles straight to the horizon. I was not prepared for a dense hardwood forest with trees so tall you couldn't see the sky. And Anne wasn't prepared for the undergrowth. She'd bought the property in late November. All the foliage had died back. She thought she had clear land.

It stretched nearly a mile to the ocean, and our first hike was a little precarious. I cut small pieces of surveyor ribbon and tied them to branches so we could find our way back. Sort of like Hansel and Gretel. And the deeper we went, the more certain I became that we'd run into a gingerbread house. Certainly there were spots of moss and fern perfect for elves and fairies.

With raspberry and wild rose bushes clawing at our clothes, the walking was not easy. But what really told me I was in another world was getting bogged down in, well, the bogs. I never knew where the term "getting bogged down" came from until my boots disappeared into this black sludge, nearly getting sucked off my feet.

Also I'd always wondered where peat moss comes from. It comes from peat bogs, just like the ones in Scotland; and being in "New Scotland" I was sure Anne had a ready-made business right on her property. I mean, the entire forest smelled thick, like a fertile greenhouse. It was really quite lovely, coming from thin dry air.

Part of all this slogging around was to find a house site. We pitched tent a few miles away and around the campfire at night talked about houses and building materials. In her mind she had a deck looking out over the ocean, and a winding trail to a meditation garden deep within the forest. She was wondering about log cabin kits, modular homes. But all this was a long ways off. First things first. After a few phone calls one evening, we had a time set to meet the general contractor, the forester and the surveyor.

Something sturdy and honest rippled off these Norwegian men, who were everything you'd expect lumberjacks to be. Huge. Burly. Yet one knew the different plants. Like huckleberry and goldenrod. Another said he'd pick and choose which trees to cut "to make it pretty like a picture." Right there I could tell Anne was smitten with the whole idea, if not a few of the men. As it turned out, so much forest made them suggest trading the wood for the road, and we struck a deal.

I left the country before the bulldozers went through; and the pictures Anne recently sent truly startled me. In one you can barely see my head above the brambles as I stumble along. Juxtaposed with that was another photo. At first I wondered why she'd sent me a picture of the main road running alongside her land. Then I realized it was on her land, right where I'd been walking. They didn't make a road. They cut a swath through a perfectly fine forest.

I still marvel that this kind of destruction is on the way to creation. And a part of me still doesn't get it, even though I know it's the only way to get a little house with a deck overlooking the ocean. In our daydreaming I put in a loft, and we both conceived a kitchen worth talking about. A kettle of stew bubbled happily on the stove and, of course, we stirred it with a spurdle, a special Scottish stir-stick sold in town. In our imaginings we even had rocks and pieces of driftwood sitting on windowsills.

Originally Anne had planned to build a camping platform, a home base she could live on during the building process.

Game for pretty much any adventure, I wondered how I'd get through security carrying a hammer.

"Don't bring anything, we'll stop at my sister's store," Anne informed me.

Finally, I'd get to see it. Years ago when her sister, Ruth bought a hardware store in Maine, it kindled all sorts of homey thoughts; and it turned out to be just as I hoped. A little country store that carried everything from hammers to bear traps to chicken and duck feed. She even sells the chickens and ducks. I wanted to stay and play hardware store, but Anne was anxious to get moving.

The thick brambles quickly changed our mind about building anything, though. "Next summer," she said, "after there's a way to get the boards to the site."

Well, there's certainly a way now—down the road. But with many more acres untouched, and looking pretty as a picture, there's plenty of places for winding trails to meditation gardens. And as things go, Anne is now carrying on a courtship via email with the road contractor. One never knows what creative things will come from complete devastation. Maybe one of these days they'll both be laying pieces of driftwood on the windowsills.

Chapter 10

Showing Off My Mistakes

All it takes to pull a remodeling job together is to have company. Not long ago my friend Kenny announced he was arriving in a few days. "I want to see what you've been doing," he said.

Great. The place was a wreck. Sawdust all over the floor, hammers, screwdrivers and drills in the kitchen. About fifteen eight-foot boards piled on the porch made maneuvering in and out of the front door a little rough. And like a fool, I said, "Sure, love to have you."

Besides having to make the place somewhat livable, I was a little apprehensive about Kenny looking things over. Of all my friends, he's the one who can really nail me by bringing up a project I once took on. And never finished.

The year was 1987. I'd moved to the middle of nowhere on New Mexico's eastern plains and lived in a shack. I mean, you could see the walls move when the wind blew, which was all the time. But I decided I wanted a greenhouse on the south side. So without measuring a thing—or even thinking it through even a wee bit—I started hammering 2x4s every which way. I had some vague notion of screwing Plexiglas on for siding, and voila! I'd have a greenhouse.

Probably because there was no plan, my enthusiasm dwindled to a standstill. Also the foundation was a little questionable. I'd thought, how simple: just attach the studs to the railroad ties outlining a small border around the house.

Well, the whole thing turned out a little peculiar, and by the time Kenny showed up, the wind had tried blowing it down for nearly a year.

"This your new addition?" he asked, raising his eyebrows as he shook the entire framing with his finger. Ever since, he never fails to tease me about my greenhouse every chance he gets. This last time was no exception.

"I want to see how your house compares with your Prairie Phase," he said.

After I learned he was coming, I went into a frenzy finishing up my paneling project. Because the entire remodel has been so pervasive, I thought it would never end. But, you know, when you're at the lumberyard and sorting through the molding, it means the end is in sight—yet I always forget the work involved getting there.

I brought ten lengths home and had to go back for more. I bought ten more and cut three wrong. Then I stained two on the rough side. And why are inventory stickers always on the good side?

Over the years I've actually had to buy a new saw or two for my miter box, so that's proof I don't fool around. Though I'm probably the only person in the world who can make a crooked cut using a miter box. There went another piece of molding. But that's OK. Toss 'em in the woodpile and in a year they make great kindling.

The hardest part is lining up molding along the ceiling with only two hands. I used lattice strips, which are pretty flimsy out at the ten foot mark. At one point I was stepping on the back of the couch and bracing my foot on the shelves, places I've told my cats they cannot go. As they watched me, I knew they were getting ideas for their early morning romps. Finally with a little bit of ingenuity I got the strips nailed.

There is nothing like putting on the finishing touches. It looked so good that I decided to trim the bathroom vanity, too. Measured and measured to be sure it was correct. It wasn't, but it looked good just the same.

So by the time Kenny arrived, the house was almost presentable. The living room is quite cozy; looks like the country cabin that it is. I proudly showed off all my work, walking him through each step of the way. And of course showing him all the mistakes. (Why do we do that?)

He didn't say anything, just looked. This made me nervous. He's one of those guys who, in three seconds, can scope out a project and have it done perfectly in five. He's pretty handy, and whatever he does seems so effortless.

Not long ago he said he was going to make a screen for sifting dirt. What I envisioned equaled something close to mine—all out of scrap lumber, a little lopsided, and when you use it your hands get cut on the edges of the wire mesh. Not his. He bought treated wood so it wouldn't warp after being left outside. He used a staple gun, and tucked all the mesh edges under a strip of wood. That's the kind of guy he is.

So as he quietly cased my handiwork, I began to worry. Was he going to categorize this, too? "Your Pecos Project" he'd call it years from now.

"It looks real nice," he finally said. "It feels good." I think even he breathed a sigh of relief.

Of course, to quickly counteract the compliment (and why do we do this?), I showed him the various edges of molding that didn't quite make it. "Guess I have a hard time making ends meet, huh?" We both laughed. He's also loaned me money.

It's a real feeling of satisfaction finishing a project. But there's always another one right around the corner. The bathroom shelves need installing and the bedroom needs a little work. I need a new door. But at least I've learned something since the days I was slapping boards together haphazardly. Putting up trim makes everything look like I know what I'm doing.

Chapter 11

High on Patching Roofs

With this dry spell, I couldn't put it off any longer. I had to patch the roof. Was it Frank Lloyd Wright who said if a house has a roof, it'll leak? Well, my house has a roof. And during the past year, various corners throughout the house started growing a bit brown. I kept trying to ignore them. Even tried telling myself I was imagining these slow-spreading stains. It's amazing what denial can get you through.

But the one leak that always got my full attention was the leak between the roof and the porch. You know, that place where add-ons don't quite add up. Whenever it rained or the snow melted, I'd fret and worry. I'd measure the severity of the storm by the size of the drips. I'd consider the pool of water by the door and worry some more. So why was this leak any worse than the others? It was right where it shouldn't be. Over an electrical outlet.

I called my electrician friend who'd installed it. His first comment was, "If a roof is going to leak, it'll be over an outlet." Sort of Murphy's Law of Roof Leaks. He merely said patch the roof, as if it were that simple.

Having no idea where to begin, I went to the store and wandered up and down the roof-patching aisle. I took a guess. Of all the brands of patching cement one was nearly sold out. I figured the people buying it knew what they were doing, so that's the one I bought along with some reinforcing tape. I was all set.

My house is tucked into the forest with only a few neighbors. We don't speak much, don't socialize. We can hardly see each other's houses. Though we keep to ourselves, we all keep an eye on things. What'd it take to get the neighbors out yakking? A woman up on her roof.

"Hey, how ya' doing?" said one man, sauntering over. "Ya know, I got real tired of patching mine. I finally had a new roof put on. Patch jobs never work for very long."

Now that was encouraging.

"Odd thing about patching," he went on, "is you never really know exactly where the water is coming in. It could come in here and start seeping in over there, twenty feet away."

I didn't want to hear that but knew he was right because a stain in the bathroom ceiling was oozing all over. I laid a long strip and hoped it worked. About a week later I decided to tackle the porch. With some experience under my belt, I was actually looking forward to it.

Except I should have chosen a different day. The weather was fine. I wasn't pressed for time. I had everything I needed. It was just one of those days where everything went haywire. The only thing I didn't do was fall off the roof, but I came close.

To start out, I put the screwdriver, tape, putty knife and scissors in a bucket. I lifted the bucket and the handle fell off. Before climbing the huge heavy homemade ladder that came with the house, I decided to pound in the rungs. They were all pretty loose. Of course, one split which meant stopping everything, cutting a board and hammering it on.

Then as I was sweeping pine needles off the porch roof, somehow the broom went flying out of my hand, through the air and hit the stone wall below. Going back down the ladder, I ripped my pants on a nail. Got to the broom and the handle had split.

Did I think about quitting? No. Despite all the warnings, I opened the can of roofing cement and immediately got it on my pants, my shoes, my shirt, and later when I looked, smeared across my face. Luckily I had my hair tied back in a bandana.

But somehow, in spite of myself, the job got done. What I finally decided to do was just go with the flow—or the stickiness—and enjoy myself. Then someone called out.

"Hey, how you doing up there?" I looked up—or down, as the case was. It was my neighbor who arrives from Albuquerque once a month. Planning to retire in a few years, he's fixing up the old family homestead. He's also stringing barbed wire around the entire acreage. This means my once pristine view of the forest is marred now by a wire fence. It hasn't made me happy.

"Doing OK," I called back hoping to at least sound neighborly. "Finished your fence yet?" I hoped he had. I mean, this fence just goes on and on.

"Still got a ways to go," he said. "Got a few leaks, huh?"

"Oh, one or two." And he went back to his homesteading.

Now this is going to sound a bit far-fetched. But it's oh-so Santa Fe. As I sat there smearing this black goopy stuff, I started thinking about fence-revenge. All sorts of wild plots came to mind, most of them involving bolt cutters and bulldozers. Then just as I got around to considering tar and feathers, what comes floating down and sticks to the tar on my putty knife? A feather.

Birds flit all over the place, coming to four feeders; and my cats kill enough blue jays to maintain a fine layer of down. A breeze stirs up the canyon every afternoon so the probability of this happening was high. Timing was all that was needed. Considering how the day started out, this little bit of synchronicity made the project worthwhile.

Now all I need to do is wait for rain and snow to see if my patch job worked. But like my neighbor said, I'll probably end up having to do it again. After all, my house does have a roof.

Chapter 12

Warm Thoughts for a Cold Furnace

Sometimes the up-keep around a place comes in ways you least expect. Like the time I had to out-wit a squirrel who'd found a way inside. His passage was the plastic dryer vent. Aluminum did the trick. And dealing with the resident raccoons certainly took me into unknown territory recently.

Four have been coming around, raiding the trashcan where I keep the birdseed. We've had a running battle for weeks. I've tied the lid, piled bricks on the lid. Nothing worked. I even spied one raccoon scampering up a tree, climbing out on a limb and tipping the birdfeeder upside down for his buddies waiting below. Their clever little fingers can do anything.

For awhile I thought they were cute. I bought some lumber for an upcoming project and one morning found a perfect little paw print on one of the boards. I even thought about preserving it with shellac.

But it didn't take long before the furry foursome quickly moved beyond cute, and I seriously thought about using the shotgun that came with the house. (Remember, this is New Mexico and just about anything goes. The man I bought the house from was presented with the gun during closing, and I was next in line.)

The day I burrowed into the crawl space to hook up the heating tape around the water pipes, I emerged furious. Someone with clever little fingers had shredded enough insulation to make several quilted beds. It meant I had a huge project ahead of me whether I wanted it or not. Desperately, I asked a friend for help.

"You want me to crawl around with tarantulas, black widows and brown recluse spiders to work with toxic materials?" he asked.

"Yeah, and don't forget the plague and hantavirus," I added, gratefully he laughed and agreed to help. Only on the appointed day he had other things to do. I didn't blame him one bit. Still, it was a two person job and I was stuck. Then I got an offer I couldn't refuse. I mean, no one has ever come forth, proposing to lend a hand.

Not long ago my friend Ken told me to line up a few projects I needed help with. Unsuspecting, the day after Thanksgiving he showed up full of pep and enthusiasm. He left nearly a broken man.

Hammer. Flashlight. Duct tape. Staple gun. Scissors. It was like performing surgery upside down. The whole operation was miserable and I tried reminding myself how grand it is owning a house. We finally got it done, but with insulation in our eyes, throats, and hair. Then I was almost sorry we'd tackled the job. Looking around down there, Ken got an idea that began fraying the very fabric of my whole life.

He wanted to get the furnace going. Said it was safer to fire it up once in awhile than to let it sit unused. It made sense, but there's this little problem. I only believe in wood stoves.

"You need to join the modern world," he said, as he's been telling me for years. But I've lived with radiant floor heating and it's too hot. I've lived with passive solar; it's too cold. I've lived with forced air and it's too noisy.

So I split kindling in the dark because I forget to do it in the morning. I've learned to live with ashes on every conceivable surface throughout the house, and for at least seven months I walk on a carpet that's continually littered with little pieces of wood. Probably, when you get right down to it, the idea of living with a wood stove is better than the real thing. And the more I protested, the less convincing I sounded even to myself. Eventually I showed Ken to the furnace closet.

"What's this?" he asked, lifting a small box.

"Oh, shells for the shotgun," I said, trying to sound casual like it wasn't my fault.

"Well, don't keep them on the furnace." He's such a practical person.

While he set about lighting the pilot, I fretted. I hadn't lived with two sources of heat in years and wondered what it would be like, how it would change my life, what new possibilities it would open. Well, two nights later I found out. I woke at two in the morning to that distinctive sound of coon capers beneath the window. I flicked on the outside light, opened the door, and eight little yellow eyes looked at me.

I could tell just what they were thinking: "You didn't have to turn on the light. We can see fine in the dark. But thanks a lot." Unperturbed, they went back to nibbling the birdseed.

For a moment I stared, hopelessly impressed. There hadn't been enough seed to spill when the can tipped over. One of them had lifted the end to slide the seed out. Their ingenuity is remarkable. Then, coming to my senses, I hissed to scatter them. That's when I decided to end the war once and for all. But instead of reaching for the shotgun, I lugged the trashcan into the kitchen.

Now, being wide awake, I decided to make a cup of tea and enjoy the deep night for awhile. But, you know, I didn't want to start a fire. The whole procedure can really get old and it takes several hours to get the house warm. So just like any modern woman I flicked on the thermostat and began thinking there might be something to say for a few conveniences after all.

Chapter 13

Y2K Ready—Or Not

Well, it's the year 2000 now. I woke up on the first and still had electricity. My water still ran. My computer still worked, and my furnace continues to keep the chill off the morning air. I'm almost sorry the world didn't come to an end. It would have added an interesting twist to things. Certainly a new perspective. As it is, I'm now faced with the same zillion things to do around the place.

When the 20th century began to close in on itself, I decided to walk around my land and do a little stock-taking. Don't get me wrong. It's not like I have a few hundred acres to consider. It's less than a quarter of an acre and walking its ragged perimeter takes about five minutes, if that. Still, every inch has some plan attached to it and as I scrambled over rocks and through the brambles I realized how far I missed the mark.

I didn't get my Y2K greenhouse built. Or the adobe wall. Or the horno. I didn't get the old chicken coop torn down. Or a shed put up in its place. I didn't even come close to adding a deck onto the bedroom. Ever notice how most remodeling jobs take place in your head? And sometimes it's the smaller projects that hold the most meaning.

Recently I decided to rearrange my main room, but it wasn't my main intent. I got myself a new desk, which won't fit the old space, which means taking apart my shelves of boards and blocks and completely redoing the entire corner.

It's sort of like making a painting to match the sofa. But surprisingly all this effort turned out to be in keeping with starting a new century.

Before I could lug the twenty-two boxes (!) of books into the studio, I had to clear a path through the studio. This was when I had a brilliant idea. I hadn't ridden a horse since I sold mine fifteen years ago. I could get rid of the saddle now. It'd been years since I played my electric guitar, which took the place of the horse. I could get rid of that, too. I suddenly began seeing parts of my past stashed here and there that no longer held true. The path kept getting wider and wider until I suddenly understood what all this was about. The desk I'm replacing dates back to a bad relationship. It's tainted with all kinds of scars. I'm ready for a fresh start.

And in the process a corner of my house that had always bothered me is getting refurbished at the same time. Only it's the type of project best reserved for summer. I had no idea wood doesn't take stain very well when the air is ten degrees and snowflakes are sputtering around. I didn't know that the grain closes up and doesn't absorb as much as when it's warm. The next morning the twenty boards I'd cut and stained didn't even come close to matching the rest of the paneling in the living room. They barely had a blush to them. Why don't cans of stain say something like if your fingers are numb and you're shivering chances are the stain won't take?

Still, I persist. Realizing I'd someday have to restain them once in place, I began hammering the 1x6s onto the wall only to discover I didn't have enough nails. This was Christmas Eve day and I pleaded with Santa to get me some nails.

I think over the years Santa has raised a few eyebrows toward me. One year I hadn't been dating a man very long and when he asked what I wanted, the answer was simple—sawhorses. He asked me several times just to be sure he was hearing right and my answer was always the same—sawhorses. Using chairs piled with books makes for a rather wobbly workspace. Well, he came through and the sawhorses have been one of the best presents ever.

Another year I got an assortment of wood screws in my stocking. Perfect. Another time a new hatchet sat gleaming under the tree. Another time a crowbar. And this year Santa came through again with a new jig saw. I'd been muttering under my breath about the cuts my old one was making. The notches I make around electrical outlets and light switches all have a slight curve at an odd angle. Yes, that's right. My curves angle. I'm not sure how I continue to achieve this amazing effect, but the true test comes soon enough. Is it the jig saw or is it me? Stay tuned. Next year Santa just may send me to carpentry school.

In my end-of-the-century reflecting and deep cleansing, I'm prone to think it might have done us a lot of good if the world had collapsed in on itself. When it comes right down to it, having enough food is a lot more important than wondering when I'm going to get around to putting a new counter in the kitchen. So now along with a zillion things to do around the place, there are a zillion new perspectives to ponder. All the hype around the beginning of a new millennium might be what we needed after all.

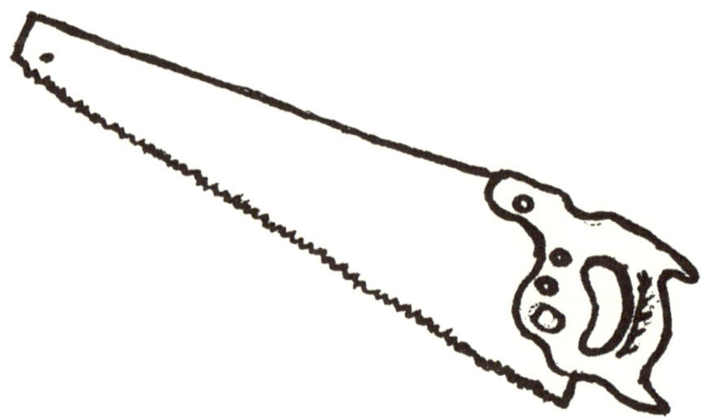

Chapter 14

I Just Wanted a New Desk

When I was in high school, I wanted to be an interior decorator. I'd rough out these elaborate futuristic houses, make paper cut-outs of furniture then spend hours placing beds and sofas into all sorts of exotic arrangements. So when I finished paneling the final corner in my living room recently, I knew exactly what to do next. Make little cut-outs of all my furniture.

Two weeks ago a friend returned a rocking chair I'd loaned to her mother-in-law. She's now moved into a nursing home so I had one more piece of furniture to consider, but the hours spent scooting little pieces of paper around buzzed with anticipation. The goal was to make room for my new desk.

I'd wanted this for a long time—more drawers, more cubbyholes, larger table area. Everything was planned. My second set of built-in shelves was scheduled to go in after the desk arrived so everything would fit custom perfect, and I was really looking forward to the work party I'd organized with my haphazard crew of somewhat willing friends. But the party had to be called off.

The desk arrived damaged.

Now, I've lived in New Mexico long enough and should have known better. I should have remembered there is hardly any standard at all, let alone a standard of excellence. If I'd kept that in mind, I could have laughed instead of cried. It was so typical, and almost exactly what happened ten years ago when I got the desk I'm replacing now.

Back then I had dismantled my work area, moved the sofa, rolled back the rug, stacked the table and chairs on the sofa—all so the desk could be delivered easily. Bring it in, set it down, and bingo everything goes back in place.

I waited and waited. One hour went by. Two hours. I finally called the store. "Oh, we're really swamped today so we won't be able to get over there," the woman said casually, as if people don't totally rearrange their lives, if not their houses, for new furniture. I mean, I had stayed home from work and wasn't salaried so I was losing money. People in "customer service" don't get that part of the equation.

Anyway, I said a few magical (hair-raising) words, worked my way to the top man, and presto the desk arrived in a flash.

The more recent scenario was similar only a lot more dire. My house was literally torn apart. In order to make it as smooth a transition as possible I'd razed everything—unplugging the computer, moving phone jacks, taking legs off tables, emptying drawers, putting stuff on my bed, cramming more stuff into the studio. A friend had arranged to pick up the old desk that afternoon.

The curtains were off the window but still on the rod and draped over the twenty-two boxes of books I'd packed from the shelves. I moved the bricks and old shelf boards outside so the deliverymen would have easy access. And when I walked back in the studio, I stepped on the drapes and left muddy waffle prints on white curtains. The path was clear, though. I was ready.

And the desk arrived totally smashed in the back. Unbelievable. But the kicker was the item had been discontinued. There might be another in stock. They weren't sure. They wouldn't know until Monday and if there was another one, it couldn't be delivered for another three weeks. Three weeks?

"Sorry," they said. Sorry? When I called the complaint department, no one would talk to me. What do you do when the complaint department doesn't want to hear complaints? They shipped me off to someone's voice mail, only the mailbox was full and couldn't hold any more messages. Click.

And this is how one of the largest furniture stores in the area, selling to all us Americans, first tried to handle the situation. It helped when three sales reps got in on it and really did try to straighten things out. It was late Friday afternoon and I'm sure at the end of the workday they gladly tromped out the store grateful for the weekend. They'd face the problem on Monday. They promised to call. And I was left with a rocking chair in the kitchen. A TV in the middle of the floor. Boxes of envelopes and mailers and computer parts on my bed. And essentially no desk at all. I couldn't put off living until Monday.

So. I canceled the order and went looking for another desk. Trouble is there is no perfect desk out there. Do people who design desks actually use them? If anyone wants to start a great business it would be making custom desks.

One office store said they could deliver in two days. Another said if I bought one that needed assembly, I could just pick it up. It beat waiting three weeks. So I picked it up. But the color was not what the salesman said it was, and by that time following thirty-seven steps to assemble thirty-one different parts (not counting the screws and dowels and hinges) was just a little daunting. My desk obsession had gotten a bit too loud. I took it back.

Luckily, here in Santa Fe we can say if it doesn't work out, it wasn't mean to be. I didn't check the charts, but no doubt mercury was in retrograde. So I cancelled having my friend pick up my old desk, moved it where the new desk was to go, and decided to try again later—when the planets are all lined up a little more evenly.

One of these days I'll again take out my little paper cut-outs and start rearranging furniture again. But, you know, when it comes to interior decorating, I really miss the words I used in high school. It was the `60s, and remember shag carpeting, swag lamps and sunken living rooms? There was something very "hip" about throwing those words around. Nowadays everything is designer this and that. What we need most, though, is designer customer service.

Chapter 15

A New Door for Mr. Ames

I decided the other day that the front door had finally had it. It was one of those flimsy doors that after too many years sort of loses its purpose. I suspect a hundred years ago someone kicked it and it never quite recovered; over time the edge of the door lined up with the doorjamb less and less. The space between the two kept widening till the only thing even vaguely holding the door shut was the latch, and even that was dubious.

I used to keep a crowbar on the front porch till I realized that was probably a little too convenient. A handy tool near a flimsy door? I could just hear someone saying, "Well, thanks, lady," as he pried his way into my house.

Over the past several months, I began thinking my cat Mr. Ames was magical or I was losing it, one or the other. In the morning I'd wake to meows outside when I could have sworn he'd been in all night. Then a few weeks ago I left him in while I went out of town for two days. When I returned, he ran up to my car all smiles; he was so glad to see me. I knew I'd left him in and looked around for any place he could have gotten out. Nothing. Then I began to wonder, did I leave him in?

About a week ago I went outside to split some kindling. Mr. Ames was asleep on the couch. I knew that. Then I heard a strange scratching sound. I looked toward the house and there he was, pushing through the space between the door and the doorjamb. He is a big cat and way too smart for his own good, and as I watched this cat-made cat door widen even more, there was no doubt it was time to replace the door.

But I'd begun hearing the call to replace the door late last fall when a bear broke into my new car. For years I'd put the garbage in my car to take to the dump the next day. On this particular night, however, things changed. At 1:30 in the morning I heard what sounded like a gunshot, then a car horn. In my grogginess I thought it was the neighbors having another one of their parties. I went back to sleep. In the morning, which was sunny and warm, I fairly danced out to my new car. I had some fun things planned that day. Then I stopped. Stunned. Was I seeing right?

The car window was broken. The rubber molding was torn and dangling. I reluctantly looked inside. Garbage was strewn from one end to another.

A bear cub, judging by the paw prints on the door, had hooked his claws into the slightly open window. One pull and the glass shattered. (The gunshot.) He crawled in (must have hit his butt against the horn on the way) and had a field day with four bags of garbage. In a matter of minutes, I'm sure, I no longer had a new car. Besides breaking the window, he bent the door and left long scratches on the side.

When I called the Game and Fish Department, they informed me there wasn't enough food in the mountains and the bears were coming down. There wasn't anything they could do. But I got some advice. "Ma'am, if a bear breaks into your house, I give you permission to kill it."

Great. With my twenty-gauge shotgun? Or with my "bear" hands?

The warden did put a rather uneasy possibility into my head, though. The smell of bananas, apples and other delectable aromas floating through the crack between the door and the doorjamb would be nothing but easy temptation for a bear. The possibility of a bear breaking in was very real. And probably this cub would invite his mother next time. Thankfully, a cold spell set in, telling all good bears it was time to hibernate. I let things go until my cat masterminded the breakout.

Replacing an odd sized door is not easy, though, especially when the only two door specialties in town don't return calls and don't answer their phones. I've never owned a retail store, but the equation seems logical enough. If you don't answer your phone, you don't make any money. So I borrowed a truck, went to Albuquerque, picked up a new door, and my handy friend Kenny said he'd help put it in the following weekend.

It took a bit of measuring and a bit of rummaging through my pile of junk wood to make things come out right.

"Ever kick in a door?" I asked him, as I held various parts in place while he screwed and hammered. He just looked at me. Kenny is the most benign, gentle person I know. He approaches the world with his heart.

"My old boyfriend did once," I went on. "He decided I wasn't the perfect woman. Couldn't get out fast enough. Ruined the door."

Kenny just shook his head.

I went on: “He also used to tell me he was more spiritual than me.”

“Maybe kicking down a door lets God in faster,” Kenny offered.

You can bet we had a good laugh at that.

Finally, the new door was in and it makes the whole house feel sturdy. It even makes winter a little more snug, too. Talk about a draft. There was nothing stopping it.

But my poor cat is terribly confused these days. Not only is the space to squeeze through gone, I got a door hinged on the other side. He’ll meow to go out and I’ll open the door. He’ll sniff the air coming through the hinges where the crack used to be and complain and complain. He just doesn’t get it. It takes some doing getting him out. Just like some people I’ve known, living with him is easy—if he gets his way.

Chapter 16

The Yarn Shop and the Lumberyard

The other day as I got ready to run some errands, I starting laughing. Where I needed to go equaled the perfect metaphor for why some men have had a little trouble with me. My list didn't quite add up. I had to go to the yarn shop and then the lumberyard. I've always moved between opposite ends and it's caused a few men to feel a little crazy. In the beginning they like this lady who can fend for herself, but in the end what they really want is someone who'll stay home and bake cookies.

Now, I like baking cookies and many times I've actually wanted to be content baking cookies. But I can only do it for so long. I blame the restlessness on my ancestors. A long line of women in my family were true pioneers, heading out for parts unknown, some in covered wagons and some even alone. The curiosity of what lies outside the boundaries has been deeply ingrained. So over the years (with covered wagons hard to come by) whenever I've felt the need to head off into the great unknown, I've usually taken on some building project.

I know tackling a new sweater pattern equals the great unknown for some women. But the complexities of fitting boards into tight places just interests me more. It's why I have more power tools than knitting needles. Still, I have knitting needles. And the other day I needed help getting a little knitted patch off a needle. I mean, it'd been twenty-two years since I knit anything and I couldn't remember how to finish, though I'm amazed my fingers even knew how to begin.

Let me explain. I'm learning to use a spinning wheel. However, my first yarns generated such snarled batches that I easily earned the fine distinction of being the worst in class. When I finally did get a full skein, it only made sense to do something with it. Which is how the yarn shop ended up next to the lumberyard on my list of things to do.

The women were kind and even commented on my yarn. "It has a...a nice texture," one clerk stammered, searching for a word that could safely define my lumpy strands. She then exercised great patience while my hands nearly contorted out of shape trying to knit two, drop one. As the piece slid off the needle, I said my thanks and headed out the door, glad I'd arranged my errands around my comfort zones.

Once in the lumberyard I breathed a sigh of relief. It always feels good getting back on more familiar ground. Grades and kinds of wood just make more sense to me than worsted and plied yarns. So I loaded up my car and headed home. When I started unloading the lumber, snow began to fall. With hardly a snowflake this winter, I was thrilled. I quickly covered the wood and hurried to the kitchen and realized I'd crossed the line again where many of my relationships have begun to wobble. Suddenly I wanted to bake cookies and quickly switched projects.

It's what winter is for, after all. Only for some reason the recipe I've used for thirty-eight years, and long before that watched my mother use, didn't work. I was so disgusted with the whole mess I threw it away, grabbed a jacket and headed outside to split some kindling. So what if it was snowing. And then it dawned on me.

As the pile of kindling began getting bigger and bigger, I realized the perfect solution to a relationship is finding a man completely charmed with a woman who is Betty Crocker one minute and Daniel Boone the next, usually without any warning. It's my inability to stay one way that makes men lose their patience. Some have even gone to great lengths to try and change me.

For me, though, the dichotomy has always been a source for inner balance as I swing between the opposing realms. It's as if leaning toward one gives the other a rest. Like what happened one Saturday morning in spinning class. By the third meeting my uneven, horribly twisted yarn was making me feel terribly inept. Then someone's wheel fell apart. The drive band, the bobbin, the flyer assembly, the whole thing just collapsed on the floor.

Grateful for a diversion, I volunteered to put it back together. Doing something mechanical offered just enough of a break before returning to the intricacies of turning clumps of wool into thin strands. Which is more magical than anything and takes a finer touch than one would imagine. This is the process of turning straw into gold, mind you; and learning to cast certain spells is not easy.

Anyway, every once in awhile my opposites come together like when I recently bought some luscious wooden knitting needles. I wanted to use them as decorations in my hair only they were too long. No problem. I'd just bought a small Japanese saw for delicate projects. In a matter of minutes I had the perfect hair decoration.

The current man in my life just laughed and shook his head as he watched me alter the knitting needles. We were on our way to a fancy dinner and I was in my best dress when I got out my saw and miter box.

I just hope he continues laughing because my lists of errands will never add up. They will never equal consistency. I need to spin and bake just as I need to bushwhack my way into and out of the woods. Men wanting a stay-at-home woman will never be happy with me. I will never be there for long. It's genetically coded. I move in a yin-yang world made up of cookies and forests. And that's just the way it is.

Chapter 17

Someone Stole My Outhouse

Someone stole my outhouse. That's right. I have—or had—an outhouse and now it's gone. It was one of the many oddities that came with the house and actually proved quite useful during the six weeks I went without plumbing a few years back. But now it's gone.

The other day I was out picking up trash that had blown up from the road. When I walked among a stand of trees and bent to retrieve a plastic bag, I thought wait a minute. Something's wrong. It took a moment or two for it to register. Then I got it. My outhouse was gone.

I actually closed my eyes and opened them again like they do in cartoons to see if I'd miscalculated. Nope. There was definitely a hole in the ground and the outhouse was missing. I couldn't believe it. Where would an outhouse go? And why would it leave? Then on a more sinister note I wondered why someone would steal it. Obviously someone was involved.

Just then the neighbor's dog came bounding up ready for one of our many walks together. Without even thinking I accused him. He's the perfect thief. He'll steal anything. To date he's taken the birdbath, assorted plant containers——wooden and clay, both large and small—— and one day I caught him dragging my ax off into the woods. If I foolishly leave a pair of work gloves lying around, he'll sneak off with one glove. I don't dare leave shoes on the porch. I've taken to keeping doggie biscuits in my coat pocket. He's easy. He'll immediately drop his thievery just long enough for me to get what he has.

As much as I wanted to blame him for my missing outhouse, I knew he couldn't have done it, though I'm sure it crossed his mind a time or two. However, I had a hunch where he'd gotten his talent.

After talking with a long-time boundary surveyor recently, I learned something very pointed. Throughout the whole state of New Mexico, San Miguel County is the most notorious for neighbors pulling up markers. Before I bought my place the surveyors came out, sighted down their lines, tied ribbons on trees and pounded in stakes. All was set. Except someone (and probably during the night) came along and followed right behind, tidying things up a bit.

Of course I immediately suspected my neighbor. I mean, there isn't anyone else around who would care, and he takes every opportunity he can to remind me my propane tank is a full 1/16 of an inch on his land, when indeed it's not.

So when my outhouse turned up missing, it wasn't hard figuring out where the problem was. But how does one handle such a delicate situation as a missing outhouse? I pondered the issue all afternoon.

Now let me backtrack a bit. The outhouse had been a source of trouble with the neighbors a few weeks earlier. One day I kept hearing a pinging outside. I looked and saw the little girl next door and her visiting step-brothers throwing rocks at my outhouse. I asked them kindly not to do that. OK they said. But I waited. I knew. Not only was I thirteen once, but I've also been a junior high school teacher. Sure enough, the sound of defiance hit squarely a few seconds later. Then quiet.

But not for long. I sneaked out on my porch and just as one of the boys heaved back ready to throw, I gathered my most searing junior high teacher voice. "You put that rock down right now." Did he? Of course not.

Then pinging started on the other side of the house. They were now throwing rocks at my propane tank. I marched out of my house and they ran just as fast as they could into theirs. I knocked and their mother opened the door. When I explained why I was not happy, she looked confused. "Why, they're all in the house," she said, perplexed that I should accuse the little darlings. (One of the things I learned as a teacher is some parents haven't a clue.)

So the outhouse had become a matter of contention with the neighbors. But how to deal with this new turn of events? Finally I decided a 'thank you' was in order.

Now this is where New Age thought comes in handy: when you think things through in retrospect. In my pondering I remembered several months before I'd actually considered asking my neighbor for help in getting rid of the outhouse. I'm sure it was an eye sore for them, and he has a pickup.

But it kept slipping further and further to the bottom of my To Do list 'til I'd nearly forgotten about it. My mind hadn't forgotten, though. In New Age circles thought comes first and somehow this particular idea of getting rid of the outhouse wriggled around 'til the event finally materialized.

I mustered up all my good neighborly manners, knocked and boldly thanked him for getting rid of my outhouse. He didn't know what I was talking about. The little girl did, though. Her brother had drug it off to the dump using his four-wheeler. What? It was hard to picture.

"I'll have a talk with him," my neighbor assured me.

The upshot is his wife, thinking it was theirs and on their land, told her son to get rid of it. She probably couldn't understand why I'd been so upset about her kids throwing rocks at her outhouse and decided to end the matter once and for all.

I've since laid a pallet over the hole and have thought seriously about putting up a fence. I'll have to be quick, though. As soon as the surveyors re-set the corners, I'll need a posthole digger ready to go. But one thing is nice. Putting up a fence will be much easier now that the outhouse is gone.

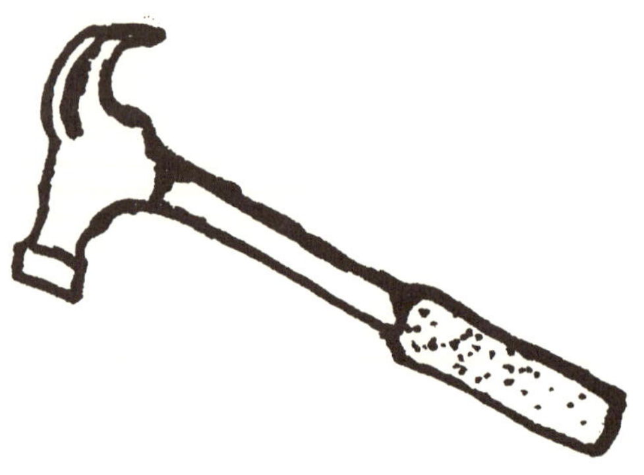

Chapter 18

A New Porch? Dream On

Have you ever walked into someone's house and wondered how they can live that way? (I'm getting to my front porch, so hold on.) Years ago I produced a documentary and remember going to someone's house to get something for some part of the script. The business details are forgotten. What I remember are the details of the house.

Newspapers and magazines were stacked to the ceiling. Boxes of old clothes lined the hallway. While walking through the kitchen, I was sure a disease was waiting to happen. Millions of plates and bowls were piled high waiting to be washed, and mold was oozing over the rims.

In the living room I had to maneuver around more boxes and bags. Electrical parts and plumbing fixtures covered every flat surface.

"My husband fixes things," the woman tried apologizing. But her voice trailed off as my eyes took in a rake leaning against a cluttered bookshelf in one corner. (I'm getting closer to my front porch now.)

I realized she was so used to the mess she no longer even saw it.

Now, I'll be honest. People have accused me of my piles. Yes, they do mount up, but they're good piles. I know what's in them and where everything is. And once a week when I clear everything away and make the house tidy again, I also make a vow to put everything away from now on. Trouble is

I come home exhausted, throw my stuff down and collapse. After a few days the piles are in full swing once again.

So (and we're finally at the porch) the other day as I came home exhausted and walked onto my porch, I tripped over the rake. What in the world? I do make a concerted effort to keep the porch somewhat tidy. If I didn't, I'd never be able to get in the door.

I looked around and knew immediately what had happened. It was that dog next door. He'd come looking for something to steal. Which suddenly explained the ball in my driveway the day before. I suspect he's now making trades. This cute little red ball for your tools. One at a time. Only the prongs on the rake got hooked on my bucket of gardening tools that fell over on the.... Well, you get the picture.

All this was perfectly timed with my friend Kenny coming to visit the next day. "You know, you need a new porch," he said matter-of-factly.

"What's wrong with my porch?" I asked, suddenly defensive of my favorite spot.

"When I sit in your living room, I feel bad that I have to look at it."

What? I couldn't believe he didn't like the pealing red paint. Or the weathered wood that has started splitting. Or the leaks, the warps, the nails that keep working themselves out from the planks as you walk on them. In its day this screened-in porch was probably really something. It's still nice on summer evenings, sitting on a wicker rocker and listening to the river. The torn screen now makes it one of a kind.

"It's the rustic look," I said.

"It needs to be torn down and rebuilt." Kenny is not one to mince words. "It wouldn't take much. Just find someone who does construction."

And here he used his fingers to put quotes around the word "construction." Yes, I know the type. But I rather like the Appalachian poor white trash ambiance around here. Yet, the more I thought about it, the more I could see a project in the making. It never fails to amaze me, though, how quickly things can get built in your head. In the throes of imagination it doesn't take much at all; when in reality it always takes more than you think—in time, in money, in worry. (Especially if you hire someone in "construction.")

The first thing I designed was a gardening shed. I decided it would be attached to the outside of the porch so I can keep all the rakes and hoes off the porch. It'll be at ground level so I wouldn't have to climb steps every time I need a shovel. Then because the mind is much more expansive than a pocketbook, I wondered why not take the new porch all the way along the front of the house. It'd be a great summer hangout. I quickly envisioned a couple of chaise lounges and tall cool drinks. (And, of course, a lifestyle with time to indulge all this).

To make this fantasy porch even more useable, I added three sets of stairs. One down to the front vegetable garden and one down to the side flower garden (as if I have time to keep one garden, let alone two). Then out of practicality I quickly added another set of stairs leading from the kitchen down to the patio dining area. Believe me, it sounds more elegant than it is.

My outdoor dining area is really a set of table and chairs arranged between several big pine trees, and renovating my outdoor eating area would probably necessitate leveling the entire hillside. Everyone who sits down for a fresh shrimp salad on a hot summer day needs to ignore the fact that they're tilting downhill. We learn to make do.

And this is where I've begun to understand the woman with the cluttered, messy house I walked into years ago. I've gotten so used to things here, I can't even see them anymore. We do get inured to the details of our own houses.

So it just may be easier to keep this new porch in my head. Besides, if I re-built it and put up new screen, what would my cat do? The biggest rip is the perfect escape hatch when the dog next door comes around looking for trouble.

Chapter 19

Remodeling is for the Birds

The other day I decided home improvement is for the birds. Not that I'm getting tired of puttering around the place or mind that I'm running out of money to putter with. It was more literal than this. My birdfeeder needed some attention.

It'd been several months since drawing a truce with the raccoons, though the outcome netted a no-win situation. Not putting out birdseed stopped the fury pests from coming around. But it also meant none of the creatures got a handout, either directly or by stealing. And for me the emptiness around the place was terrible.

How sad to look out and see empty feeders. Even more, how disheartening to watch chickadees hopefully pecking for seeds. Something needed to be done.

The latest buzz-word in building these days is "greatroom." All of us who live normal lives, live in normal houses and have normal incomes have living rooms. Those positioned at the other end of things now have greatrooms—big rooms that spill beyond the usual confines of kitchens, dining rooms and living rooms. Greatrooms often combine all of these into one.

Within these definitions my living room isn't great, but it is wonderful. What with the paneling finished and as many shelves as one wall can hold, the homey feel couldn't be better. But since rearranging the furniture, the great part of this wonderful room was gone: watching birds at the feeder.

That for months there were no birds at the feeder is another matter.

What bothered me even more was not being able to see the tree. I used to watch its branches fill as birds approached the feeder. Now I could only see the forest. Which, of course, explains my whole life. Other people can't see the forest for the trees; but I've always enjoyed looking "out there" instead of "right here." After all, details can get so banal. Laundry, groceries. They have a way of making us believe that's all there is, that there is no forest, no larger picture. But in this case I was willing to let the forest go. I wanted the details back. I wanted the tree.

And the changes I made were all due to a Steller's jay.

I heard him squawking in that annoying way they have and it wouldn't let up. Good grief. I walked to the window and there he was——big, blue, and arrogant and hanging on with all claws to the trim around the porch screen and screaming his head off. Then when he saw me, he quickly hopped to the feeder, back to the porch, back to the feeder, all the while shrieking and cocking his head my way.

Now, I have a biologist friend, Bernd Heinrich who has made a name for himself studying ravens. Scientists, as well as all us nature observers, are supposed to take an objective view of goings-on in the forest. We're not supposed to project human behavior on other creatures so I know Bernd will not take my report too kindly. But clearly that jay was screeching at me: "Do you get it, lady? We're hungry."

Yeah, I got it and since I spend more time at my desk than on the couch and there's a big tree out the desk window,

I decided to move the birdfeeder. Simple. I mean, how difficult can it be switching a feeder from one tree to another? But as usual it turned into one of those projects that takes all morning. Changing the rope and rigging up a pulley system wasn't the worst of it. The aggravating part was dealing with that dog next door.

He seems to have an eleventh sense about when I set things down. He can be miles up the canyon sniffing fence posts, but as soon as I lay a hammer down he immediately comes lurking through the shadows just waiting for me to turn my back.

I call him Ruff. It's not his real name, but from his coat to his disposition Ruff just fits him better. It especially titles his thinking ability. He continuously displays a rough time navigating through the simplest ideas. Except when it comes to stealing.

I filled the feeder, went to get the ladder on the other side of the house, heard the phone ring, ran in to answer it and looked out the window. I hadn't seen Ruff all morning but there he was: walking away with the birdfeeder.

"Ruff! Ruff!" I called, picking up the receiver before I'd even said hello. It happened to be an editor of a national magazine and here I was barking at her. I quickly explained the dog next door was stealing my birdfeeder. "He's in the tree?" the woman asked incredulously. Not at all understanding the situation, she proceeded to talk at length about the article I was working on. I tried being professional and business-like all the while more concerned about where my birdfeeder was going.

When I finally ran outside, neither Ruff nor the birdfeeder were anywhere to be seen. But thankfully I know my fairy tales. Just like Hansel and Gretel he'd left a steady stream of birdseed trailing behind as he drug the thing off into the forest. When he saw me coming, he started moving faster, a gleeful grin spreading across his menacing face. I reached into my pocket for the only ammunition I keep for such occasions—dog biscuits. He immediately dropped the birdfeeder, undoubtedly thinking I was rewarding him for his little game. It's only one of the reasons why I call him Ruff.

Anyway, things finally became normal and I can safely say I'm once again enjoying a tree, the chickadees are happy and my notion of a greatroom has returned. There's nothing more wonderful than having a birdfeeder right outside a window. The best thing that's happened, though, is the jay has stopped yelling at me. And that's worth the price of birdseed any day.

Chapter 20

Men and Their Missing Closets

Things were getting a little too tame around here. I was getting that itchy feeling. Had to do something. So I started moving to the other end of the house looking for a project. Picture me sneaking down the hallway, crowbar in hand, and you got it right. A bit of demolition always livens things up. But I had no idea where this urge was taking me until one morning I woke and knew immediately. It was time to redo the closet.

Now that may sound dull, but there's a story here on several levels. First, at least I had a closet. During the early '80s, I hung out with a crowd of budding architects, builders, and engineers in Santa Fe. Not sure how I fit in, but there I was. And one fine day an architect in the group had his grand unveiling. It was his first house and we all showed up.

The one other woman and I strolled through the house. We could hear the men oohing and aahing. "Way to go, man. You did it!" went the general hoopla. But we weren't so sure. Something wasn't quite right. A few more pass-throughs and we got it. We found the happy architect standing in the patio.

"Looks great," we said. "Only problem is there are no closets."

His face fell. I'd never seen such a look of terror. Sure enough, he'd forgotten one crucial selling point. Closets. There was no place to keep clothes or linens, an ironing board or extra food. And it was way too late to go back to the drawing board. Now, keep in mind this man is one of the hot-shot designer/builders in town these days. He really has made it big. But whenever I see or hear his name, I remember how he started. No closets.

Another time I went to an open house in White Rock. The man selling it had built it, and his sales pitch proudly boasted solar this, adobe that. But again something felt wrong, and this time it didn't take long to figure it out. Sure enough, no closets. And when I mentioned it, there was that look again. Sheer terror, like he'd been caught.

What had finally caught up with these men was indeed being found out. They were disconnected from the feminine and it showed. They had no idea how things were done in a house. No woman would have forgotten to include a place to store pillowcases—probably because we've always been the ones to go get them. But judging by the amount of storage space showing up in men-designed houses these days, I must say men are finally coming around. All us mothers, wives, girl friends, mistresses, daughters and sisters are finally being listened to.

The second part of my closet story hooks into a childhood phobia. I was in fourth grade, and one evening went to get my pajamas out of the closet. As I slid one of the doors back, it slipped out of the track and dropped straight down. On my big toe. A solid half-inch slab of plywood falling at least two feet is not light. Even today my body remembers the searing pain.

I'm sure you can imagine the drama of the moment; and oh, the attention I got. My mother even drove me to school the next day because I could barely walk. I got to wear a sock on one foot and that garnered even more attention. Even kids who didn't like me gathered around. Everyone wanted to be in the know. It was really quite lovely, and to be honest, worth all the pain.

But a distaste for all kinds of sliding doors—shower doors, room dividers, cabinet doors—became deeply embedded. Even roll top desks and sliding lids on breadboxes give me the heebie-jeebies. Anything that slides. So it was no small matter, forty years later, when I decided to smash the closet. It had sliding doors. I'm sure my gusto rose from some kind of revenge, and I took to the project with complete joy. I loosened a few screws on the tracks then grabbed the crowbar and went to work. Disappointingly, it didn't take much. The entire demolition took all of ten minutes.

Now what to do? When my father took off the sliding doors after they fell, he re-configured them onto hinges. I decided to live with my open closet for awhile and soon realized I didn't want any doors at all. The room is so small that any hint of added space is welcome. But just leaving my clothes open to the world, didn't work either. I wanted at least to tuck them away visually. The solution was quite simple. I bought some off-white fabric and made curtains. I made a valance, rigged up a wooden dowel, attached the curtains to wooden rings and the whole assembly works fine.

It's also become a great hiding place for my cat, Mr. Ames. It's not unusual to reach for something in the closet nowadays and suddenly have a cat paw snag my ankle. He loves holing up behind the curtain, ready for the attack. Then he'll get that crazed look, start weaving in and out of the folds of material then roll around playing with the hem. He's forever forgetting he's over four years old now and should show a little more dignity. But how can he even think about propriety when the closet is now open to all those shoelaces? Each pair of shoes sports one end of a lace completely chewed to a pulp. But what's a few laces when a huge fluffy cat who reigns King of the Forest looks so cute acting like a kitten?

So I'm learning to live with a new closet these days. There are still a few things I want to add, like one of my famous shelves, so I'll carry on. But in the meantime, I can't help but wonder. Whatever happened to this now-famous builder's first house, the one without the closets? Considering the whole house was about the size of some of these walk-in closets today, I'm tempted to call and find out. I may be pleasantly surprised to find his feminine finally came out of the closet.

Chapter 21

There's Nothing Like a Good Find

The other day I was fussing around in the yard when some friends stopped by. About two years ago Barb and Joe bought one of the little shacks near my house for a rental and last year began remodeling it. They've ripped out everything that could be ripped out and replaced all the doors, windows, walls, counters and floors. I used to work with Barb when I was a teacher and I've enjoyed having them in my neck of the woods on weekends. They stopped by on their way to the dump.

"Have anything you want thrown out?" they asked. I hate going to the dump. I rank it on the same level as putting gas in my car. A necessary bother. So I scurried around, gathering garbage, ashes and cardboard boxes. As I threw the stuff in the back of their truck, something caught my eye.

"You taking those old boards to the dump, too?" I asked.

"You want them?"

Now, there's nothing I love more than junk wood, unless it's how it comes to me. I'd put the thought in the back of my head awhile ago that I wanted to make a cold frame. But I sure didn't want to buy any wood for it. So the thought, I thought, sat idle. But as things go, this little thought didn't pass through but got busy stirring up all the threads it needed to make wood for a cold frame appear.

We unloaded the wood—nice planks of 2x10s in varying lengths. I quickly calculated, if worked right, I wouldn't even have to cut them. The boon buoyed the rest of the day. There's nothing like a good find.

I'm not sure when scrounging for wood took hold for me, but I've always enjoyed making a haul, whether it's picking up dead branches and twigs in the forest behind my house, snagging drift wood in the river or stopping alongside the road for logs that have fallen from trucks. Once I squealed to a halt and grabbed a wooden crate from the middle of the highway. It splintered beautifully and made great kindling.

My father was a boat painter. He worked down on the docks and was always bringing home scraps of junk wood from old hulls and decking. Undoubtedly I inherited this trait from him. We had a fireplace when I was growing up, and he was forever adding to the woodpile behind the house with what came floating down the bay. Paint has changed since those days and I rather miss the blue and green flames from lead based enamels. The kindling I collect isn't near as grand as those old boards; but if my father were still alive he would be quite proud of my pile of junk wood. He'd know something worthwhile got passed on.

Growing up poor, he was a great scavenger of just about anything, not just wood. And every Tuesday mornings he'd start for the alley on trash day to check out the neighbor's cans. Sometimes I'd go with him and we'd bring home all kinds of neat stuff. When my sister first married, she showed her husband a wooden handled umbrella she'd found in the neighbor's trash. It was in perfect condition. Poor Marc; he was deeply humiliated to realize he'd married a woman who thought nothing of going through people's trash. But she, too, had inherited the trait. My father was philosophical about it.

"You can find anything if you look for it," he used to say. And this certainly held true for my cold frame. After the planks arrived, I needed a window. But not just any window. One with panes, and I stored the thought in the back of my head and went about my days. As luck would have it, I got an assignment to do a story about the Re-Store in Espanola, a place for recycled building materials. Not one to miss a good deal on anything used, I quickly toured the store. Tucked in a bin was the perfect wooden paned window and all for $3. There's nothing like a good find.

About five years ago I had a landscaping gig at a gallery near the plaza. As I was trimming back the Lamb's Ear and laying some bricks for a pathway, I heard that screech, screech that's so distinctive of nails being pulled out of old boards. It went on and on. Finally, I went to check it out. The people who owned the café next door were redoing the upstairs deck.

"Hey, can I have those boards?" I called, ducking out of the way as they tossed them over the balcony.

"They're all yours, lady," one of the workmen called back.

This was before I moved to where I live now and I'd been looking for some make-shift walkway to keep me above the mud. Now I had a gangplank to the door. Perfect. Then when the people next door moved and said I could have their flagstone, I replaced the decking and used the boards for flowerbeds.

When I found a deal on used bricks at the Salvation Army, I outlined a pathway into the orchard. When I moved, I brought the bricks, the flagstone, and the café decking with me—along with wood I'd salvaged from the river that I eventually sawed into pieces for a miniature coyote fence to outline another flower bed—and to keep out all those little coyotes.

I'm forever rearranging my finds and the outside of my house can nearly be likened to a garden of found objects. When I moved here, I dug up about fifty paver bricks that had sunk below the surface. My friend Kenny finally asked if he could have them. He had a project in mind. I said sure; and his face just brightened. I knew the feeling. There's nothing like a good find.

Chapter 22

Betty and Her Chicken Coop

It's not enough that I get harassed out here by all the bears, raccoons, birds and the neighbor's dog. Now the lady at the bank is on my case.

When the new bank started up out here in Pecos, it didn't take me long to switch my account from all the big conglomerate takeovers happening in Santa Fe where they couldn't even keep track of deposits accurately. There's nothing like small town living. People know you by name, and one of the young tellers even knows my account number. Can't ask for better service than that. Unless it's asking Betty not to give me such a hard time.

"Hey, why didn't you tell me there's a place I can get used building materials?" she wailed at me through the drive-up window after a story I did about the Re-Store came out. "We're building a chicken coop and need a door and a window."

The thing about Betty is she's the perfect example of not judging people by their clothes. When I see her, she's in her bank manager outfit. But the day she told me she'd asked Santa Claus for a cement mixer and a log splitter—and got them—I knew she was far from what she appears. This lady knows what work is.

The other day she invited me out to her place to see the chicken coop. Now, I also have a chicken coop and I was expecting something like mine. There haven't been chickens in it in years. The man I bought the place from said it was there when he moved in. And it became another item on the list of all the extras that came with the house like the twenty-gauge shotgun, the impossibly heavy homemade ladder, and the outhouse, which was stolen a few months back.

Of course, all these extras were supposed to make me feel like I was really getting a deal, but the one thing that caught my eye was the chicken coop. Yet I don't understand chickens and my only experience with a chicken coop was when I roomed with a woman in a house in the hills behind Santa Fe. Our landlady had chickens and said we could get eggs any time we wanted.

Well, one afternoon Anne and I decided to go get some eggs. I'm not sure how it happened, but somehow we got locked in the hen house. I can't even remember how long we were shut in before our landlady came to check her flock and found us, too. However, I do recall it was not pleasant having those chickens glaring at me the way chickens do.

So with this vast experience with chickens, I gamely went to see Betty and her coop. And was totally impressed. It measures 12x16 and is stronger and better built than my own house with ceiling joists, rafters, braces—the whole bit. It's divided into two sections. The feeding area is enclosed with—what else?—chicken wire. Another area (where the door and window Betty was looking for will go) is for the nests. She anticipates three shelves of nests.

When she gets off work, she goes home and starts on the coop till her husband can help at the end of the day. Of course she showed me her cement mixer, of which I was sorely jealous. Then she showed me the slab she poured. The floor is smoother than another friend's slab, and he's a contractor. These chickens are going to live in style.

"I just love sitting out here and listening to their peep-peep-peeping," Betty said as we stood and watched the twenty-two baby chicks peck the ground and soon my outstretched finger. I found myself wondering again about my own chicken coop. It really wouldn't take that much to repair. It needs a new gate, and whoever built it nailed the crossbeams to some trees, which have grown and taken the roof with them. It's definitely fixable, but do I dare take a chance against all the critters out here?

Another nudge to fix it up comes from Kenny. He loves my coop, dilapidated as it is. He's always saying I should get some chickens—not because he wants them, but because part of his whole philosophy about life rests on chickens. He grew up in Lowell, Mass. and says all the neighborhoods had chickens, and as a teenager he used to deliver milk in these neighborhoods.

"It was outlawing chickens in cities that caused the demise of communities," he insists. "People who had chickens talked over the back fence. People don't do that anymore because they don't have chickens." I get a little lost following his logic, but certainly I'm one for bringing back rural amenities. I mean, I like hearing the rooster down the canyon in the mornings. The peacock I can do without.

When I got home from Betty's, I went and stood in the middle of my chicken coop and wondered. It's pretty basic. The hen house is an old dog house with a hinged door. The tin roof is a bit leaky. But the chicken wire seems pretty solid all the way around. The only things in it are all my esoteric books from graduate school. Surely, I can do away with those now.

So I think Betty has given me an idea, though I have a better one. Get her up here to fix my chicken coop since she's so experienced now. More than anything, though, I'm looking forward to the time I can go to the bank and buy fresh eggs. Nothing like living in a small town where chickens bring the neighbors together.

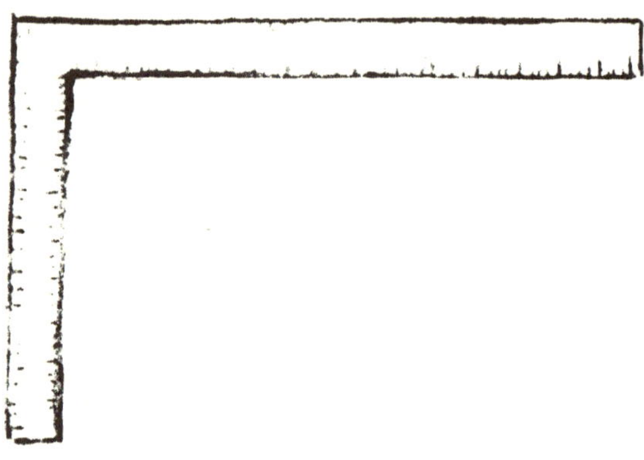

Chapter 23

Let the House Burn: Detachment

Ever since I was a little girl I've been afraid my house was going to burn. The prevailing thought in Santa Fe would say I "came in with it" from a previous life, that I'd experienced a house burning and carried the fear with me. Wherever the fear came from, I used to keep a paper bag of doll clothes next to my bed so I could grab it on the way out. Every day when I finished playing with my doll, I'd put the clothes back in the bag by the bed and the doll in my bed.

Funny, when I ended up leaving my home in Pecos last week because of the threat of fire, I didn't even think about those doll clothes and my doll, and I still have them. This may be my only clue that I've reached adulthood. I turn fifty tomorrow.

Actually, I've been looking forward to this for oh, about fifty years now. I've always enjoyed my birthdays. And this one is a turning point. For one thing, I've made it. It's been a long haul and my graying hair and wrinkles attest to it. Another clue that I'm on the verge of coming of age came during the fires.

We weren't told to evacuate, but fires burning at either end of the Pecos Canyon one night made me feel terribly boxed in. Sirens raced up and down the road, helicopters thump-thumped overhead. It was a bit unnerving to say the least, so I decided to leave. I suspect for a long time people will continue pondering what they would take if they had to evacuate in ten minutes. A girlfriend had to leave White Rock and had a little longer than that—about eleven minutes. She took journals, jewelry, her daughter's favorite toys and some clothes.

I wandered through my house, grabbing genealogy notes and old photos, my great grandmother's quilts and cut crystal bowl. Next came important papers, then manuscripts I wrote before computers and therefore aren't on disk. I took a handful of clothes. After this, there was a very odd feeling. When it came right down to it, nothing was really all that important.

And this became more of a turning point for me than turning fifty. Then again maybe this came about precisely because I have lived half a century. I've had a ton of jobs, lived in a zillion houses, and been through enough divorces and relationships to know nothing is permanent. As I wandered through my house, I realized if it went, having a house that burned would be one more phase—like when I raised sheep in 4-H. Like the time I lived in my tent in the Colorado Rockies. Like the time I wrangled horses in Arizona. Like the time I left my home state alone and went looking for a small town where I could settle. Definitely, another phase was finding that small town and becoming a waitress in a truck stop.

So with fires raging nearby, I walked through my house and realized I could leave it because it isn't me. Even though I love my house, knowing I could let it all go turned into a very satisfying feeling of detachment.

I've put a lot of energy, time and money into fixing this place up. But having the house destroyed would never take away what this place has meant. I moved here at the end of a horrendous relationship, and turning a dilapidated shack into something livable has been an act of healing, a true rising out of my own metaphorical ashes.

And speaking of ashes, I've been hearing a bit of humor rising from the real ones lately. It runs along the line of, "Well, it needed to be remodeled anyway." I thought about this. What a perfect way to finally get the house the way I wanted it: let it burn and start over. Then again, you don't really know what you'd do until you're faced with it.

One man I know was thinking about leaving Los Alamos and moving to Santa Fe. His house burned. How convenient. Now he could move without having to move all his stuff. But he's decided to stay and rebuild. Others who thought they'd grow old and die on The Hill are moving. You just don't know.

It's been a rough few weeks, and like others I'm back home in among some very dry woods. Something has changed in me, though. When I left, I chose not to take any books. I'm obsessive about books—or thought I was. Within a matter of seconds I realized the books I've read are still in me, and the ones I haven't, well, they aren't. My photos and writings are still at a friend's. So if the house goes, I can just walk away.

On second thought, I just might get out those doll clothes and put them by my bed. I'd hate for them to burn after all this time. So I guess if I'm going to save my doll clothes after all, I better look around for some other clue that I've reached adulthood.

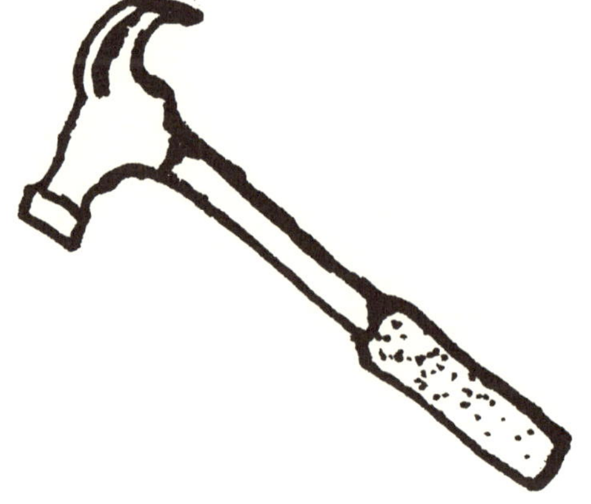

Chapter 24

It Might Burn So Why Bother?

How handy. Now that I've evacuated twice so far this summer, my house is a tad empty. Now I can get to some of those walls I've been meaning to refinish.

The second time I had to leave, that weird feeling arose again: nothing was important. I'd taken all that couldn't be replaced the first time. This second time seemed futile. But my friend Ken was here and since we had time, though it looked like the fire was on the backside of the ridge behind my house, he became more practical. This time I took books—lots of them. And since I'm keeping them at his place until we start getting drenched with rain, corners in my house are much more accessible.

When I put more shelves up last winter, I didn't want to stain them until I could leave the windows open. Now most of the shelves are empty and I can certainly let the air in to circulate now. So that's on my list of things to do. And the wall in the bedroom where all my old family photos hung is also now empty.

I'd been meaning to panel that wall for a long time, but didn't want to take the time to take the photos down. Isn't it amazing when you start putting off a job, the more arduous the task becomes until you can barely move? For years I didn't want to take down those photos. Too much work. But as sirens raced up and down the canyon one night, it took all of about five seconds to get those photos down. Amazing what a little adrenaline can do.

My friend Barb called not long ago. She lives further up the canyon and one recent evening we shared evacuation stories. She and her husband Joe travel to Mexico every chance they get and come back with masks and other artifacts they hang on their wall. They also collect paintings.

"I can't believe how dirty our walls are," Barb laughed. "They haven't been painted in ten years, but I didn't think they were this bad." Now instead of paintings and such they have white squares and splotches on their walls. They're also keeping their valuables in storage until the drought passes. We got about six raindrops a few days ago, so it'll be awhile.

Another wall I've been eyeing for a remodel is in my kitchen. The top shelf holds all my favorite cookbooks, that is it used to. "You want any of these?" Kenny asked, standing there with a bag and ready to fill it that ominous afternoon.

I took one look and nodded. I like to fancy myself the great chef, though most of the time I whip up veggie burger mix and let it go at that. Still, I have hopes I'll find time to follow recipes again. My favorite cookbook? Betty Crocker's slick page spiral bound notebook style. Not because my tastes aren't highly refined these days, veggie burgers excepted, but the cookbook has a story.

I was nineteen and wanted to be a stewardess; and an airline flew me to their main office in Minneapolis for an interview. I have no idea why I wanted to be a stewardess. I think it had a lot to do with the idea of sashaying down the aisle in a cute little uniform. I didn't get the job, which air passengers can be eternally grateful for, but I stayed a few days and went sightseeing. One of the places was General Mills. At one point I'd even considered being a home economist and was so fascinated by the tour, I just had to get a cookbook. So that's how Betty Crocker has come to achieve high prominence in my kitchen. We're on a first name basis.

But now with the cookbook shelf bare it's possible to consider taking down my brick and board shelving system and putting up something real. The only question is does it make sense?

If I and others in the canyon are storing our goods elsewhere because our houses might burn, what's the sense in painting walls, or making built-in permanent shelves? It's a weird state of limbo these days. The weather is perfect. Paint and stain would dry quickly. Our houses are stripped and ready for all sorts of remodeling and sprucing-up projects. But our hands are tied. Why bother if the houses might burn?

So I've turned my energies to my garden, that poor patch of weeds out front. I'd just planted some new flowers before I had to leave. Not being able to come back home to water left things in a very sad state. And the other day I planted more flowers, again wondering why. I might have to leave again on any given moment.

Barb is busy in her garden too, also wondering why. Of course, one of the things we're both doing is raking pine needles trying to clear a firebreak. I only have a quarter of an acre, not much land unless you're raking it. And living in the middle of a forest creates a lot of pine needles. But as trying as the task is, it did seem worthwhile the other day as helicopters flew over carrying water buckets again. Luckily they got the spot fires out.

So. My house is nearly empty. My land is nearly clean. It's been an exhausting summer. One of the things I like to do each summer is make a really tacky canned peach pie. Can't even do that anymore—my Betty Crocker cookbook is in storage.

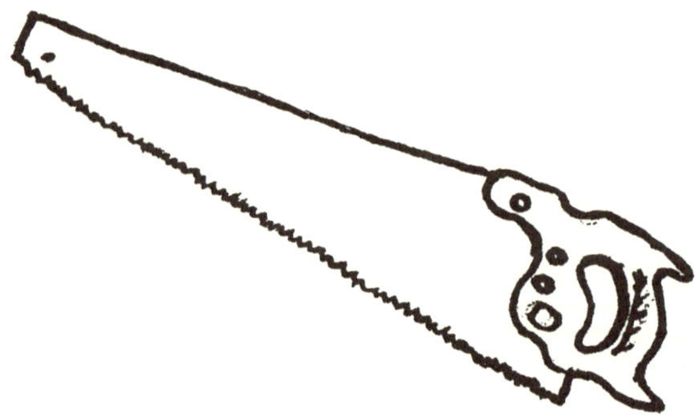

Chapter 25

The Joy of Tossing Around Ideas

After I told Kenny he could have all the old concrete bricks I'd dug up in my yard, he began telling me about some plans he had in mind. He wants to switch his home office with the spare bedroom because it's bigger and has an outside wall.

"So what's an outside wall got to do with anything?" I asked, not really paying attention. We were sitting in the sun at my house and I was getting deliciously lazy.

"Well, I want to take out the window and put in some French doors," he said casually.

"And they'll open onto a patio?" I asked hopefully, my attention suddenly stirring back to the present. His side yard is sheltered from the neighbors by a brick wall. It'd be the perfect place for a little intimate sitting area. Quickly we were off and running with ideas.

He had pen and paper and hastily sketched as we talked. I leaned back and closed my eyes to better envision this new patio. "You'll have to take out the raised railroad tie flower bed," I said, "and take out the dirt to ground level."

"Yeah, that's a good idea," he said and went back to sketching before adding, "Then I could just move the bed down a bit."

"Why not take it out completely, make a low stone wall that would encircle the tree and become the edge of that walkway you've been talking about. You could really open the space for a bigger flower area."

Kenny loves planting flowers. He always has bouquets of flowers in vases on the table; I knew I had him.

"Hmmm. I hadn't thought of that," he murmured. "I like it."

As I sat in the sun, I was stunned. This was a momentous occasion in my life. For the first time I was suggesting ways a man could re-do something around his house without him getting all weirded out.

I can't even remember the number of times various men in my life (and there have been more than one or two) have mentioned some remodeling project they had in mind. Being who I am, I immediately jumped in with suggestions of my own, ready to get out my hammer. And they immediately backed off, not from the project, but from me.

It's always been fun to plan and talk about remodeling. But men seem to think it's a scheme, a devious way to move right in—as if that's what I want. What they didn't know is that even as a kid I drew house plans, and the journal I've kept for forty years has pages and pages of house plans in it. None of which will ever be built, I'm sure. But some of the ideas are just great, if I do say so myself.

So when Kenny started talking about taking out a wall, I did what I normally do—jumped right in. And he didn't back off. He listened. He drew. He added ideas and I added more. It was really fun.

Then I said: "You know, I don't think there's enough space for double French doors. They'd be out of proportion with the wall. Why not have one paned door with a stationary glass panel."

Then I realized this was an old, old idea. My second husband and I built a house and the upstairs loft had two rooms separated by a paned door with a stationary glass panel. At the time, I had just taken up stained glass and designed a series of five panels for the space. After I finished the first one, he said, "You'll never finish the rest." Not real encouraging, and to make a long story short, after we got divorced I continued working with glass. And ten years after his snide remark, I actually finished the last panel. (Obviously, I hadn't worked on them every day.) And just to be the little witch I can be, I wrote him saying he'd been wrong (again). I had finished them.

I've since given up stained glass, but still have the panels and several years ago was all set to make a room divider so I could put the panels in them. But I moved. So while Kenny and I sat in the sun, I told him about the panels, now safely tucked away. When I finished, he quietly sketched a stationary panel for my stained glass and I breathed a sigh of relief. My stained glass panels will finally have a home. And it's perfect that they'll be with Ken.

For some reason he has always collected my weird cast-offs. Once when my husband and I were moving, Kenny came by to see how we were doing and noticed a pile of pottery in the trash. "Things from high school and college," I explained. He reached in and pulled out the most hideous ceramic bird.

"We can't turn this loose on the world," he said. And whenever he's moved through the years, I've always checked. Sure enough, my high school art project is prominently displayed. He has other oddities of mine as well because, according to him, humanity needs to be spared. They're all art projects, which gives you some idea of my talents. But I'm glad my stained glass panels will finally be safe and displayed like they were meant to be. It's not every day a person can find a home for all those misinformed creative urges you just hate to throw away.

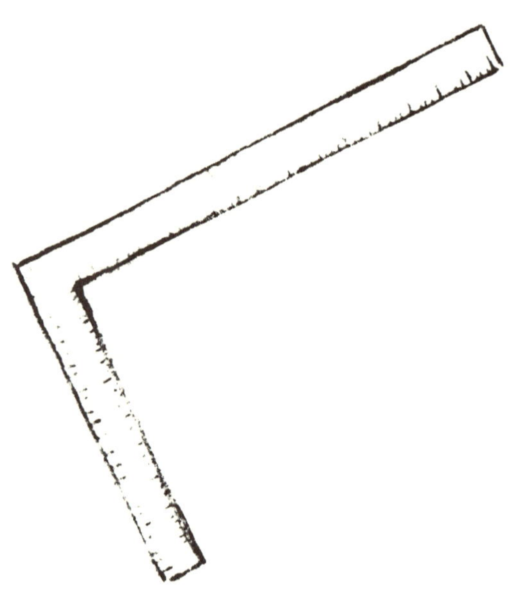

Chapter 26.

A Garden of Miniatures

My garden is about ready to make the world's record. Reporters will be arriving by the busload any minute. No matter what I do, no matter what plants I put in the ground here, everything gets stunted. I have a garden of miniatures.

Three years ago I planted some yarrow. Happy the first year, it shot up two feet. Last year proved the same. I thought I'd finally found a plant that could survive here. But this year all the stalks measure about eight inches.

Years ago a friend's mother gave me some kind of shrub. It transplanted well but never quite lived up to the long stalks it came with. It just puts out these little stubby twigs then sprouts very healthy leaves. Same thing with my lilac bush. I wanted a huge bushy thing on the corner. It's been four years and it's still about 18 inches tall but sprouting all kinds of runners with little lilac leaves coming up all over. Clearly, having a huge bushy thing on the corner is not going to happen.

When I bought this place I had in mind a wonderful lush garden with all kinds of long stemmed flowers waving in the mountain breezes. Not a chance. Not only is it a garden of miniatures, it's a two year garden. It must take about two years for roots to hit the adobe because that's about when they stop.

I planted some white and pink cosmos this year. Lovely. They blow in the wind just like I wanted. But I better enjoy them now because in two years they'll be about four inches high.

Still, I continue fussing with this garden. My latest ploy in trying to turn the front yard into something you'd actually want to look at is finally getting rid of the wild roses. This statement is full of contradiction, though, because there is no way to get rid of wild roses. They thrive on abuse. Cut a root and two bushes will grow. They're kind of like worms, regenerating from tiny segments. This may be why I keep finding worms in among the roots. They understand one another.

Over the years dealing with these roses has meant altering portions of the garden. Following the incredible maze of roots necessitates moving rocks and realigning terraces. And this year is no exception. Only this time they are leading me to a project I've put off and put off.

I like summer because I like sitting in my garden under the morning sun eating watermelon. And for four summers I've wished a little patio would get built. As I ripped and yanked at some rose roots the other day, I suddenly realized the patio is now in the making.

In following a gnarled tangle of half inch round roots, I had to tear apart a line of big rocks that outlined the future patio space. Over the years I hacked at the roses whenever one would show its pushy little head, all the while thinking someone ought to dig up those roots before a patio goes in.

Well, it looks like "that someone" is finally getting the job done. Took her awhile. But everyone knows good help is hard to find these days.

Isn't it funny how everything works out as if there was a plan after all? Once the momentum began for the patio, a contractor friend called. "You want some bricks?" he asked, knowing full well I don't turn down offers of leftover building materials. He brought over a stack of gray flagstone last summer; that along with the brick will probably be just enough for the patio.

It always works this way. About twelve years ago when I was a teacher out on the plains, I turned a barren patch of dirt into a lush garden. One day I needed some flat stone for a patio. And lo and behold the father of one of my students came by that very afternoon asking if I wanted some stone. I hauled away every piece of limestone he had and it was just the right amount for the space.

It's gardening that let's you know magic is still around.

I already know it'll be next summer when the magic will truly show itself. The patio will be done and it will be the perfect place to sit in the mornings. It'll also be then that I won't mind that all the plants in my garden are dwarfs. In fact, I know I'll be pleased.

Because I won't have an eight foot lilac bush out front and yarrow shooting up to the sky, I'll be able to sit in my patio and still see the forest. The forest is the reason I moved here. So I guess there is something to be said for miniature plants after all.

Chapter 27

Always Within the General Idea

Recently I gave a friend directions to my house: Turn left, turn right and travel down the road until you see a garden all torn up. Can't miss it. Place is a mess.

I've continued digging up those tenacious wild roses; and with the yard literally uprooted, saw no reason not to dig up the grass where I wanted to put the brick. And with everything else dug up, there was no reason to put off any longer what I'd been putting off for four years. Let me back track.

If you recall, I gave my friend Kenny some concrete bricks I'd dug up in front of the house. There were at least a hundred. This lengthy excavation was the first project I undertook after buying the place and somewhere in my little brain I'd decided they had sunk.

Now I see it was all a ruse on my part to deceive myself. Those bricks didn't sink. They were buried. And I've only now come around to admitting this. And I've only admitted this because all the flagstone slabs I replaced the bricks with are nearly gone. But they haven't sunk. The silt from the mountain, from the road, from my driveway covers them a little more with each torrent of rain.

I've stood at my kitchen window and watched thin layers of mud swoop down and settle in my yard. It's exactly how deltas get made.

So one rainy day I gamely tried sloughing off water with a trench. It worked somewhat. Then I constructed a more intricate ditch system—one going this way from the mountain, another going that way from the road, and a third cutting a diagonal across my driveway. But the best one of all angles water down toward the neighbor's. I mean, it's only fair. If I have to listen to their teenage son's booming "music" at three in the morning, they can use a little more water.

Ah, the justifications that surface in a neighborhood.

Anyway, one day I watched a trail of water travel a path as if it knew right where to go: Cut through the trench, channel along the garden, curve down the driveway, turn here, there, and in one great sweep curl around the corner of the stone wall and rush into a standing puddle by the front door. That filled, wash down stream over the flagstone.

I realized my flagstone is in the path of least resistance and the perfect place for the water to dump its silt. Actually, when dry it does look kind of pretty—little caked ripples of mud shining with flecks of mica. This mixed with perfect paw prints from my cat, Mr. Ames, makes for some astonishing images.

Spontaneous art aside, I knew I couldn't put it off any longer. Another retaining wall was necessary, and I decided to make it by extending a footer for a stone wall outlining the bricked-in area. Plans for a footer began and one weekend when my friend Kenny was visiting, I was all set.

"I've never made a footer," he admitted, following me out to the garden.

"Oh, they're simple," I said.

"Well, Modesto has hired an entire crew to widen his driveway and it doesn't look simple," Kenny countered. Modesto is his next door neighbor.

"Don't worry," I said. "My way is easy." And I commenced to telling him where to dig and how deep, then went rummaging through my woodpile. I set pieces of junk plywood in the trench, backed them with rocks, pushed mud (read adobe) against the backs to hold them in place. It looked like an old fashioned make-shift sluice early miners used for panning gold. We were done before breakfast.

"That's it?" asked Kenny.

Now, my footers are not your usual fare, but they work. Nothing is quite level and the width varies considerably. But they are solid and that's all you want because all the unevenness will get covered once you slap on the mortar and stones.

Kenny raised his eyebrows in doubt, but didn't say anything. Until I went to his place one day and chanced a peek over the neighbor's wall. There was Modesto's crew measuring, stretching string, everything in order and ready to go.

"They sure are going to a lot of trouble," I said.

And Kenny in his growing wisdom said: "Yes, they still have a few things to learn."

The goal is pretty basic. You just have to keep the concrete in the space where you want it to be. No need to get fancy with 2x4s and stakes and survey lines.

Years ago I watched a contractor pour a slab and that's how I got the general idea which, of course, is how all of my projects are: always within the general idea.

Epilogue

Not long ago I ran into a woman at a party. Through my columns, she'd been following my activities here at the edge of the forest. We got to talking and she told me about a wall she was replastering; I told her about my stone wall. "You mean you're still working on that?" she asked incredulously.

"Well, yeah," I said feeling a bit defensive. After all, I don't do this stuff fulltime. But I couldn't blame her for being surprised. I've been writing about my stone wall for a long time and working on it even longer. We chatted a bit more then moved on to other conversations with other people.

Later I got to thinking. What does all this mean—all this fooling around with wood and cement, stains and brushes? And especially my stone wall? There had to be a purpose, some point to all this madness. It took a day or two to arrive at some semblance of a reason, but I got there.

Unlike other things in my life the goal of all these projects is not necessarily to finish them. And the perfect book that helps vindicate my endless hours of tramping along the river and through the woods to find the perfect stone is *Stone Work*. Author John Jerome takes on the task of dismantling one of those New England boundary walls made of stacked stones. When he decided to move it from one side of the property to another, he anticipated: "I'd get inside this elemental task, examine it, master it. I'd take my time at it, take years if necessary…such a gradual approach, I proposed, would move it out of the realm of drudgery."

He's right. Once out of the realm of drudgery, anything can take on an aura of being more than it is. And this, I've decided, perfectly explains my projects. They lighten the bleak side of the daily grind. Oh sure, they offer an excuse to get out and use some muscle and get away from the computer, but fixing faucets, mixing mortar, cutting boards is more like playing. And I know exactly where this came from—my father letting me freely play with his pliers and hammers, his wires, saws, screws and rasps.

I spent hours building little tables and chairs for my dolls. In the end they all leaned (literally) more toward modern sculpture than anything useful, and I'm afraid that sometimes my building skills haven't progressed much beyond this. But that's OK. It was nothing but sheer amusement then and that's all it is now, a diversion from drudgery.

I've also made a promise with myself. If working on my stone wall ever starts feeling like a burden, I'll just finish it and be done. But it'll never happen because I'd never have anything to talk about at a party.

About the Author

Throughout the West, Cindy Bellinger has done it all—wrangled horses, taught ballet, waitressed in a truck stop, modeled for artists, painted houses, tended gardens, taught school, and in her more daring moments broke a wild horse and took flying lessons. No matter where curiosity and challenge takes her, for twenty-five years she's written about it. She also publishes the *Woolly Times*, a magazine for fiber people and their fiber animals. She lives in Pecos, NM.